The Illusion of Happiness:

CHOOSING LOVE OVER FEAR

A Spiritual Novel by Ken Luball

& Bodhi ("A Spirit Guide")

Author's Note:

"What is the Meaning of Life?"

The Meaning of Life,

The reason we are alive,

Is to Listen quietly to the Spirit within and

Follow the path it leads you on.

There are four books in "The Awakening Tetralogy":

"Today I Am Going to Die: Choices in Life"

"The Spirit Guide: Journey Through Life"

"Tranquility: A Village of Hope"

"The Illusion of Happiness: Choosing Love Over Fear

Spirituality is the belief there is a piece of God (a Spirit or Soul) within every life and, because of this each life is Important, Equal, and Connected.

My goal writing these books was to try to *Awaken* and help others, who are *Awakened,* more fully understand what *Enlightenment* is, so their Journey Through Life may be more fully realized.

Three of these stories are written in the first person, following the "Spiritual" Journey Through Life of a child, as they learn the lessons needed to answer the question above in an understandable, interesting, unique narrative, which is not only thought-provoking but engaging as well.

Bodhi is my *"Spirit Guide";* he is able to easily communicate with me as I write down his thoughts. Though my journey towards *Enlightenment* is not yet complete, *Bodhi,* being a *Spirit Guide,* most certainly is *Enlightened.* We wrote this book for all those seeking to begin the *Awakening* process *or* have *Awoken* and seek to venture further on their path towards *Enlightenment.*

It is only with Bodhi's love and support

we were able to write these books "together."

Learn more about each of the four Spiritual books in this tetralogy

at my website: http://kenluball.com

Table of Contents

Dedicated to the Children of the World

We are dedicating this book to the *Children of the World*. It is our hope your parents, and others who love you, will read this book, and by doing so, be able to help you choose your path through life wisely. It is our wish your journey be filled with love, happiness, and wonder.

Prologue:

To the Children of the

World

As you are growing up, you will notice life can appear

To be very challenging.

The world is not always a very nice place to live in.

You will see many things that make you wonder

Why bad things happen to so many.

You will see people who do not have enough food to eat

Or a place to live, and others,

Who do not like someone because they are different.

Unlike the picture above, regardless of what color your skin is,

The country you live in, your name, religion,

Or any other differences there are,

It is important you do "Not" believe anyone is better

Or more important than anyone else.

"Every Life is Equally Important",

Regardless of any perceived differences there are between us.

Living a good life has Nothing to do with the job you have,

The amount of money you make,

If you are famous or anything else you may hear about

When you are growing up.

Rather, the only important thing is that you are a "good" person.

Be someone who cares about others feelings,

Helping them whenever you can,

Treating everyone with kindness and love,

Even if they do not treat you that way.

You will find there are many in the world who are unhappy,

Afraid and worry only about themselves.

Please, do "Not" be like them.

You can change the world if you simply "listen"

To the quiet voice in your heart and

Share that message with everyone.

Embrace life with awe. Be kind to everyone.

Share the goodness in your heart with those who are different or

struggling.

And, most importantly, treat others

Like you want to be treated.

If you do this, you will be happy.

~ 4 ~

Choose "Not" to live in a world where everyone is afraid,

Worrying only about themselves.

Instead, care about others, be generous, empathetic, loving, respectful,

humble, patient, honest, compassionate, kind, positive, grateful,

hopeful, and optimistic about life.

Be courageous; care about others feelings,

Be friendly and help them if they are different or in need.

If you do this, you may find your life will be happy and meaningful.

The path you choose through life will decide

The future of the world.

The older generations have "Not" done a very good job

Taking care of our planet and each other.

It is up to you, therefore, to make the changes

That must be made,

By choosing the "right" path in life.

"Your vision will become clear

Only when you can look

Into your own heart.

Who looks outside, dreams.

Who looks inside, awakes".

Carl Jung

Chapter 1:

Finding Your Light

The answers we seek, to "Find Your Light",

Enabling us to embrace Inner Peace, Love and Meaning in our Life,

May "Never" be found in the world by looking outside.

They may only be found by looking "Within", where the Spirit exists.

Many of us intuitively understand this.

To accept and allow your Spirit to guide

Your Journey Through Life, however, is quite challenging.

This is due to the dominance of the Ego (Self).

The Ego is everything we were "Taught" and "Believe" to be true since

our birth.

"Awakening" begins when we start to question everything we

"Learned".

"Enlightenment" happens when we "Accept" as truth

Everything we learned was "Wrong".

The journey is long, difficult, and often lonely.

The "Meaning of Life" is pursuing this journey,

"Sharing Selflessly"

With all others your "Light" within.

"Why we are Alive"? What is the "Meaning of Life"? These
questions have been asked for millennia; it may be surprising how simple
the answers actually are. When we are born, these answers are already
within us. In fact, it is not until "*after"* we are born the answers to these
questions become lost in the many challenges we all face in life.

"The first five years of every child's life is the most important". It is
during this time they learn what is expected of them and how they will

react to different situations in the world. It is also when they will develop an overall view of the world and how to treat others. Their opinions, prejudices, beliefs, and aspirations are often formed during these early formative years and will form the basis of how they will act and treat others throughout the rest of their life.

During these years, if a child is taught to view the world and others through a *Dark Negative Prism*, one where *"Fear"* dominates *"Love"*, then the challenges they face will be great. By looking at the world this way, they will learn to be concerned only for themselves, rather than for everyone. By embracing this view, their Journey Through Life will often be lonely and their struggles abundant.

If, however, during these early years, they embrace *"Love Over Fear"*, then their lives will take a much different direction. By embracing the primary importance of *Love*, they will begin to understand life a different way; one where there is concern and compassion for *"Everyone"*, rather than only for themselves. These children will learn to understand and treat others with respect and view life with *wonder* and *love*, rather than with *fear* and *hate*.

"What is Learned during the first five years of a child's life, may

affect their entire life." The many struggles we have throughout our lives are often a result of the beliefs we developed during these early, impressionable years. We *Learn* about our relationship with the world during these years and then may spend *the rest of our life* trying to undo the harm that was done. This harm is caused by the *Acceptance* of the many false self-centered egocentric messages we received as the truth, as we *learn* our role in the world. By the time a child is ready to begin school, these messages are often so ingrained within the child, they influence their every thought and action, *oftentimes for the remainder of their life.*

I would like you to picture an open suitcase. Before we are born, the suitcase is empty. With our birth, though, *the "Self" (or Ego), which is everything* we *"learn", and "believe to be true", after we are born,* begins to fill this suitcase up. With each interaction we have, the suitcase becomes heavier, as it begins to become cluttered with the baggage we accumulate, from all the erroneous things we have *Learned* during our lives. The heavier the suitcase becomes, the *dimmer our Light* gets and the more we will have to unpack when we *Awake* and begin our journey toward *Enlightenment.*

In the suitcase are *all the false self-centered truth's Learned by the Self and Accepted by the child* as they are growing up. Though it does not take very long to fill the suitcase, it may take the rest of their life, if at all, to *"Find Their Light" again*, unpack the suitcase and return to the inner peace and understanding they once knew before the suitcase began to fill; before they were exposed to the many untruths *Learned* by the *Self* and *Accepted* by the child as real. The heavier the suitcase they must carry, the more difficult their *Journey Through Life* will be and the harder they will have to search to *Find Their Light* again. Let us therefore strive to make our Children's lives happier by making their suitcase lighter, so they may *"Find Their Light" within* earlier in their life.

Most of our suitcase is packed in the earliest years of a child's life, from the moment of their birth to 5 years old. We then, often, spend the rest of our lives trying to unpack what we have accumulated.

As we search for our "Light" and begin to question the truth of all we were taught during these years, we begin to *"Awaken"* and start the arduous task of emptying our suitcase. As our suitcase begins to empty, our *Light* begins to shine a little brighter each passing day. It is not until our suitcase is almost empty, though, that the *Light* within will again be found and *"Enlightenment"* is discovered. Since the *Self* will always remain with us until our death, the suitcase will never totally empty, though our *Light*, not quite as bright as it was before we were born, is now becoming quite luminous.

We may spend our entire life trying to unpack the suitcase we mostly filled during the first 5 years of our life. The more the suitcase fills and the heavier it becomes during these early formative years, the more challenging life will be. As we get older and are faced with the many difficulties life will present us, the more difficult it becomes to unpack the suitcase. When we are an adult, often we are just trying to survive in the world and have embraced the *Self's* self-centered path through life; this makes emptying the suitcase much more challenging.

Imagine if our child's suitcase remained mostly empty as they grew up and *Learned* the mores of society and how to survive in the world. It is possible to raise our children like this, to lighten the suitcase they must carry and keep their *Light* shining brighter throughout their life. To do this, however, there must be a change in our paradigm, teaching our children, especially during the earliest years of their life, to embrace *"Love"* rather than *"Fear"*.

It is therefore essential, to keep this damage to a minimum, to keep their *Light* shining brighter, by raising our children in a *positive loving* way, teaching them to trust and follow the guidance of their *Spirit within* from the moment of their birth. By doing this, our children will help usher in a shift of consciousness, which will change not only the direction their lives will take, but also the trajectory of all life on earth as well.

Many spend their entire life undoing the harm they experience in the first 5 years of their life, as they are socialized to accept the traditions of society. It is our hope this damage may be kept to a minimum and, by doing so, make it easier for them to *"Find Their Light"* once more.

The answers we seek, to "Find Our Light", enabling us to embrace inner peace, love and meaning in our life, may "never" be found in the world by looking outside; they may only be found looking "within", where the Spirit exists.

Sharing your "Light" with the World

It is much easier to accept the status quo,

Recognizing the numerous problems experienced by many

As inevitable, having little recourse to help others.

Look at the world today and throughout history

To see what Living in such a world is like.

It is a world of Fear, Hate, Prejudice, War, Hunger,

Homelessness, Climate Change, ad infinitum.

Every person Can change the world.

We each have, "Within" us, the Means to do so.

It begins by "Listening" quietly, "Accepting"

The messages you "Hear"

Then Sharing your "Light" with the World.

Chapter 2:

Introduction to the

Mind, Body, Spirit

Connection

The Failure of Psychology

Has Psychology truly embraced the Mind, Body, Spirit Connection?

Current practice often treats only the two-dimensional Mind and Body,

Ignoring the Spiritual contribution to disease.

Though Counseling and Medications may allow someone

To be able to cope and survive in the world,

It ignores "Fully" treating an illness,

Allowing it to return more readily.

"The Spirit gives our lives Meaning".

Without its inclusion in any treatment,

Only part of an illness will be treated

Leaving the treatment incomplete.

Though the Spirit cannot be scientifically proven,

And may not be readily accepted by the Psychiatric or Medical

community,

In truth, neither can the Id, Ego or Superego Freud postulated.

Yet its premise is readily accepted in Psychology.

It is time for many in the scientific community

To widen their view treating *All* illnesses by

Equally by including the Spirit

Along with the Mind and Body.

"Awakening" begins with the recognition the two-dimensional mind, body connection does not answer gnawing doubts *within* that question the validity of *everything we have been taught.* *"Enlightenment"* occurs with the realization everything we have learned in our life, we had accepted as true, *"Was Not"*. With *Enlightenment*, the importance, acceptance, and addition of the *Spirit, is now added to the mind body connection.*

What is the Mind, Body, Spirit Connection? Much has been written about the connection between the *Conscious Mind and Physical Body.* By adding the *Spiritual Soul* into the equation though, a whole new world of possibilities is opened. *Spirit* cannot be discussed using just science, medicine, or psychology; that is why this book will focus primarily on the *Spirit* to help us all better understand exactly what the *Spirit* is and how it may help us better understand the *"Meaning of Life"*.

In this book, when we discuss the *"Ego"* (*"Self"*), it will be from a *Spiritual*, rather than a psychological point of view. As described in the previous chapter, our definition of *the "Self" ("Ego"), is everything* we *"learn", and "believe to be true", after we are born.* To further simplify this discussion, we will consider the terms *"Self"* and *"Ego"* as synonymous.

According to Sigmund Freud there are three parts to the human personality; they are the Id, Ego and Superego. The *"Id"* is the basic, primal part of our personality, that is present from birth; it allows us to get our basic needs met and satisfy our basic urges and desires. Next, the *"Ego"* begins to develop during the first three years of a child's life and helps us make sense of our thoughts and the world around us. Finally, the *"Superego"* starts to emerge around the age of five and is the ethical part of our personality, providing the moral standards by which the ego operates. Since this book is dealing primarily with the *Spiritual* and not the Scientific psychological aspects of our personality Freud discussed, *we will use the term "Self" to represent all three parts of the human personality, "the Id, Ego and Superego combined", rather than differentiate each part of our personality individually.* We are doing this to decrease the confusion that may arise if we get too technical or specific and to simplify the ideas we are trying to present.

Just as Freud talked about the Id, Ego and Superego, perhaps it is time to add one more category when considering the complex behaviors and emotions of people; that category is the "*Spirit*". Since *Spirit* cannot be seen or proven to exist using science alone, there needs to be a *"Spiritual Leap of Faith"* to accept, not only does it exist, but it is important to both our emotional and physical well-being as well.

If we can accept the "*Ego*" ("*Self*"), then why can we not accept the "*Spirit*." Both cannot be proven scientifically, yet many theories and treatment of different psychiatric illnesses are based on "helping" the *Ego* (*Self*) adjust to the chaos and confusion it is exposed to in the world. The *Spirit* is simply there to help balance out the *Self,* and unlike the *Self,* which is rooted in "*Fear*", the *Spirit* is rooted in "*Love*". Perhaps if we also begin to treat illnesses, by including the *Spirit* in the healing process, new improved avenues for treatment may be discovered.

Chapter 3:

The Wall, the Mask, and the Door

The Facade

The Facade disguises the "*Real*" person,

Hidden in plain sight, hiding behind a *Wall and Mask,*

The Ego "Taught" us to use to "Protect" us

When we were children, not only from everyone else,

But from ourselves as well.

We only begin to truly Experience life

After the *Wall and Mask*, the outer shell of pretense,

Is stripped away,

Leaving our "Authentic" Self

To share our Love Selflessly with others.

Part 1 – The Wall

The *"Wall"* is an invisible barrier set up by the *Self (Ego)* to "protect us" from the stressors of everyday life. It often forms when we are children, and its strength is reinforced throughout our lives as we are exposed to the chaos and other harsh realities of life. The *Wall* is erected around the *Spirit* by the *Self* to protect us from many of the negative emotions and pain found in the world around us. *To help with visualizing the Spirit and Self, to make this easier to understand, imagine the "Spirit existing within our heart" and the "Self existing within our mind."*

The *Wall* is a barrier that not only keeps out pain but, at the same time, encapsulates *the Spirit within our heart*, preventing and muffling its purpose, as well as the brightness of its *light* throughout our lives. The stronger the *Wall* is, the more dominant the *Self* will be and the less we will be able to "hear" our *Spirit within*. Unfortunately, though the *Wall* protects us, it also prevents the *Spirit* from thriving, dimming its *light* throughout much or all of our life.

The *Spirit* represents *"Unconditional Love", which is love that is shared without expectation of receiving anything in return*, and all the positive emotions we associate with happiness and serenity; these inherent emotions cannot easily penetrate the *Wall*, inhibiting the *Spirit's* influence. Though we may find the *Wall* helpful in our lives to "protect us," we pay a price for its continued existence. By containing and imprisoning the *Spirit,* and therefore allowing the *Self* to set our boundaries, we are not free to truly experience love, happiness, or other positive, uplifting emotions. The *Self* may give us the *"Illusion"* of love and happiness, but these impressions are mostly false. *All "learned" emotions are a Mirage; though they seem real, they are not.*

The emotions associated with a truly "happy" meaningful life come from the *Spirit* (our *Higher Self*); if the *Spirit* is imprisoned behind a *Wall*, its message will not be clearly heard. Another more *Spiritual Enlightened* way of putting this is, your *"Light"* will be dimmed.

Almost everyone erects a *Wall*, some stronger and thicker than others; it is much easier to put up the *Wall* than to tear it down. *This Wall is often present in many people who have been diagnosed with depression or other psychiatric, psychosomatic, or medical illnesses.* In fact, these illnesses could be, at least partially, a result of the *Spirit* trying to break down and penetrate the *Wall*, trying to change the direction of our life, but our *Self,* using *Fear*, *"to cause these illnesses,"* preventing it from doing so.

While living primarily through the *Self* may help us survive in the world, it will often not give our lives meaning or allow us to find true happiness. There are many examples of this throughout history. There are people who appear to have everything, are wealthy, "happy and successful", yet they cut their lives short by falling prey to suicide due to the pain they feel *within* every day. This pain, often caused by the inability of the *Spirit* to thrive because of the *Wall*, reaches a point where it can no longer be tolerated. In order to treat this pain, therefore, it is important to not only treat the symptoms of the pain, caused by the *Self,* with counseling and medication, if necessary, but also to spend time trying to break the *Wall* down, so the *Spirit* may thrive as well. Continuing to ignore the *Spirit*, by treating only the symptoms of an outward illness as a consequence of our exposure in the world, will not produce an adequate or lasting result. It is only by the inclusion of the *Spirit,* a complete long-lasting treatment may be formulated. It is only by penetrating the *Wall*, the *Spirit* may also thrive, and the illness be *fully* treated.

The Self allows us to survive in the world; the Spirit, however, gives meaning to our lives and allows us to embrace life more fully. Surviving is not enough. Though we may live a complete life, die of old age, have a family, friends, money, and more, when we are close to death and we look back on our life, what are we going to see? If our life was dominated by the *Self*, due to the *Spirit* being imprisoned behind the *Wall*, will we feel we have lived a meaningful life? If, however, we have been able to break down the *Wall* "protecting us," allowing the *Spirit* to have a significant influence on our lives, we then will have experienced the positive inherent emotions emanating from the *Spirit* and been able to connect with others on a *Spiritual*, rather than a superficial, level. Then, when we examine our life as we prepare to die, there may be a very different, more positive conclusion.

Before we are born and exposed to the chaos of the world, there existed only the *Spirit,* which is eternal. The *Spirit* represents *Unconditional Love*: happiness, peace, and all other positive emotions. After we take our first breath, however, the *Self* comes into existence as well. The *Self* is there to help us "survive" in the world. Though the *Self* will always be an important part of our life, to help us navigate and get by in the world, *it is the "Spirit that gives our lives meaning."* On an *Enlightened* level, the "purpose" of life is to realize and *accept* this, and by doing so, allow the *Unconditional Love* of the *Spirit,* we first experienced before we were born, to return and be shared.

The most interesting and ironic thing about the *Wall* is, though it is usually erected when we are children, we often spend much, if not all, of our lives fighting to break through its confines. The *Wall* smothers us, preventing the *Spirit's "light"* from shining brightly. By dimming this *light* from *within,* our ability to experience the many positive pure emotions that come from the *Spirit* are muted. When we *Awaken,* the first cracks begin to appear in the Wall; with *Enlightenment and the Acceptance of the Spirit Within,* we finally break through, destroying our *Wall.* We are then free to experience what we were destined to feel, *the pure, inherent positive emotions of the Spirit.*

For the majority, however, though the *Wall* may be thinned, we may *never* fully get rid of it. Instead, there is a lingering feeling something is wrong, but we often do not know what it is. The resultant frustration may lead to anxiety, depression, or a number of other illnesses, psychological and medical, as our internal conflict between the *Self* and the *Spirit* continues throughout the rest of our life. By breaking down this *Wall*, the immense potential of the *Spirit* will not only be freed but will also be able to shine its *light* brightly, as it was always meant to.

There are many who wonder what an *Awakening* and *Enlightenment* are. They feel, to experience these, are the reason we are alive. *"Awakening"* is the *realization* of what we just talked about, the importance of the *Spirit* and freeing it from its confines. *"Enlightenment,"* however, is the *Acceptance* of this, thereby freeing the *Spirit* from its imprisonment behind the *Wall*.

Many *Spiritual* books have been written, many saying similar things; they only say it in different ways. Reading and knowing something are different, though, from *Accepting* it. With the emergence of an *Awakening*, which starts when we begin to *question everything we have learned,* the first cracks in the *Wall* begin to appear. Reaching

"*Acceptance*", though, involves completely breaking down the *Wall*, allowing ourselves to be vulnerable to the uncertainties and "pain" in the world the wall "protected" us from, and, by doing so, releasing our *Spirit* from its captivity. By freeing our *Spirit* and *accepting* its message of *Unconditional Love* and the pure, positive feelings and emotions it contains, *Enlightenment* may be achieved. If our *Wall* is still intact or even if it is just weakened, then though we may be *Awake* and able to understand all we have talked about, *Enlightenment* will continue to elude us.

W*hy are we alive?* We maintain it is *to Awaken* and become *Enlightened*, to free our *Spirit* from its confines behind the *Wall*, so its message and *light* may be shared with all. Success is not prestige, wealth, or anything else associated with the *Self* or the outside world. *Success, as we maintain, is freeing the Spirit by Awakening, breaking down the Wall, becoming Enlightened, and Sharing this knowledge and Unconditional Love (Your "Light") with all others.*

Part 2 – The Mask

In addition to the *Wall*, which the *Self* erects to "protect" us, we also learn how to hide our feelings behind a protective "*Mask*" we all wear.

~ 27 ~

This *Mask* is an imaginary metaphorical *Mask* we wear over our face, one we wear to hide our feelings and emotions from others. As we grow up, we learn how to create and wear this *Mask*. This *Mask*, which cannot be seen by others, is used as a disguise to hide our feelings, so others will not know how we really feel. For instance, we are wearing an imaginary *Mask* when we act like everything is fine when it is not, saying we do not care about something when we really do, pretending to be nice when we are upset, or acting angry when what we really feel is hurt.

This list could go on ad infinitum; by wearing a *Mask*, not only do we *mask* our feelings, but we also *mask* our "real emotions", which emanate from the *Spirit*. By doing this, we mute our *Spirit's light* and its message to others and ourselves. We even have medications that will help us *mask* our feelings as well. There are prescriptions for depression, anger, stress, anxiety, pain, and many other "illnesses" prevalent in society today. However, these feelings are what make us who we are, allowing us to reach our full potential, and define our very being. We experience them for a reason, and by hiding them behind a *Mask* and treating them with medication or counseling, we stunt our emotional and *Spiritual* growth. *By wearing these Masks to hide our feelings, we imprison our Spirit and light within our heart.*

We all wear Masks. While some are only partial and cover just a portion of our face, there are other *Masks* that cover our entire face, preventing anyone from seeing anything behind it. *Masks* help us survive in the world and allow our responses to different situations be socially acceptable. The larger the *Mask* and the more of our face it covers, the greater the stress and anxiety we experience and feel. Besides taking multiple medications to help treat our stress and anxiety, we also develop many subtle coping mechanisms as well, which help us survive every day.

Many of us, especially those whose *Masks* cover their entire face, become very adept at hiding almost all our feelings from others and, often, even from ourselves. Some are so good at this, we may see a "happy, funny, successful, wealthy person with a prestigious job, wonderful family, and many friends", one day go home and end their life. To everyone in the world, this comes as a shock, as we wonder how someone who "has everything" could do this. This person may have been on medications to help them cope and receiving counseling as well, yet their unhappiness, stress, depression, and anxiety may have proven too much for them to bear. It is not easy to continually wear a *Mask*; therefore, they may need to seek help by trying other ways to numb their pain. Such people often turn to drugs and alcohol to help keep their *Mask* intact. To everyone around them, they may appear gregarious, but within, it is all an act. They were so good at wearing their *Mask* and hiding their emotions, absolutely no one, even those closest to them, could see behind it.

For most of us, though, our *Mask* is a partial one, covering only part of our face. Though all our emotions are not hidden, and there may be instances when we are able to take off the *Mask* for a short period of time, we always know the *Mask* will always be there to "help us" if need be. With our superficial everyday encounters, it is just easier to wear the *Mask* to help us get through the day. We become so used to it, most of our interactions with others are superficial. All others see is what we project to the world, hiding our real feelings behind the safety and protection our *Mask* provides. Though this survival technique is useful and allows us to "get by," it also hides and prevents anyone from getting to know our "*true selves.*" Besides others we know superficially, *the Mask even hides our Higher Self or "Spirit" from those closest to us as well.* Just as the *Wall* imprisons our *Spirit* within our heart, the *Mask*, which metaphorically covers our face, imprisons our *Spirit* behind it as well.

Our problems are amplified exponentially when we are so good at wearing our *Mask*, even those we love and care about deeply cannot penetrate it. Though we try very hard to "open up" to our family and close friends, we are often afraid to do so. We have become so adept at protecting ourselves by covering our face, we are unable to allow and free our *authentic Self*, our *Spirit*, to shine through. For many, this is a daily battle, only made worse by the many stressors we encounter.

This disconnect, between who we really are behind the *Mask* and what we project to others, is the cause of much of the unhappiness, depression, and anxiety rampant throughout the world today. If we define happiness as success in the world, then this happiness is *"conditional and an illusion."* If, however, we describe happiness as success *within*, freeing our *Spirit* (*Higher Self*) from its confines behind the *Mask* and the *Wall*, allowing our *light* to shine brightly and our *"authentic"* self to reveal itself, then this happiness is *genuine* and may be shared with all.

We have all seen "successful" people, like the ones described above, who are anguished, searching for happiness in the world. We have also seen others, who are considered unsuccessful by society, due to their lack of money and material possessions, who are truly happy. The former, who the world at large considers successful, still have their *Mask* on and their *Wall* intact, if not at least partially. The latter, however, have been able to rip their *Mask* off their face and shatter the *Wall* surrounding their heart; they are free. Their emotions are not *learned*, but rather are *inherent* and come from *within*. Their *Spirit* has been freed, and in being able to do this, they are able to experience life authentically, as it was meant to be.

Part 3 – The Door

Imagine a hill with a *Door* on the top. On one side of the hill, at its base, is our very dominate *Self.* When we are here, the hill is very steep and difficult to climb. As our *Spirit's* influence becomes a little stronger and we begin to *Awaken*, though, the incline of the hill appears less severe, and we can begin to ascend it in an effort to reach the *Door* on the top. We know if we can reach the *Door* and go through it, we will find *Enlightenment* on the other side, "*becoming one with our Higher Self (Spirit).*"

We struggle every day to reach the top of the hill. Some days, we approach the *Door* only to find ourselves unable to go through the doorway, instead slipping back down the hill we just climbed. These highs and lows experienced every day, often multiple times a day, dictate how hard it will be to climb the hill. Every "once in a while," though, we pass through the *Door* and get a glimpse of *Enlightenment* on the other side, a warm, bright *light.* Unfortunately, the stress and anxieties of life soon return, and we find ourselves being dragged back through the *Door* once more, falling back down the hill.

Sometimes, we may fall only partway down the hill. There are other times, though, we fall all the way back to the very bottom of the hill and must begin our ascent again, once we are able to. *Falling in and out of Enlightenment, going back and forth through the Door, is common as we Awaken and begin our journey towards Enlightenment.*

This is very frustrating for us, though, as the glimpses we have of *Enlightenment*, of the inner peace and love experienced on the other side of the *Door*, compel us to try to remain there. However, circumstances in our lives, along with our *Self*, continue to pull us back through the *Door* and down the hill. We know *Enlightenment* exists, yet we are unable to fully embrace it and remain on the other side of the *Door*.

At this point in our discussion, it is important to take a step back and examine the circumstances that cause this to happen. If we learn and understand how the hill was formed, as well as the reasons we have such difficulty climbing it and going through the *Door*, then perhaps we may find a way to make the hill less steep and the *Door* easier to pass through.

To understand this, we must go back to the very beginning of our lives, even before we were born. In the calm, warm, peaceful darkness of our mother's womb, as we begin our life, our *Spirit* begins its journey as well. The *Spirit* is eternal, *Within* every life and it accompanies each life through its journey. As we develop, before we are exposed to the harsh realities of the world, when only the *Spirit* is present, there is no conflict or any negative emotions. There is only peace, *Unconditional Love,* and all the inherent emotions we will identify as positive after we are born. This calmness and peace we feel is "*Enlightenment.*"

From the moment we are born though, with our first breath, everything changes. From that very moment, the *Self (Ego)* is formed. Everything we see, learn, and are exposed to throughout our life will help strengthen the *Self,* determining many of the challenges we may face *Awakening* and finding *Enlightenment* once more.

Throughout our lives, we are "socialized," taught how to act, treat others, and survive in the world. We are taught by our parents, siblings, friends, teachers, clergy, TV, movies, books, the internet, and more about the difference between right and wrong, good and bad, how to act and treat others, our prejudices, the need to "look out for ourselves (*self-love*)," the importance of money and having material things, and how to find "happiness" and "success" during our life.

We observe and become immune to the horrors and impacts of hate, prejudice, and fear. Instead, these negative emotions and more become internalized and a part of our "DNA." The degree to which each of us is exposed varies, but its effect on each of our lives is profound. In learning how to survive in the world, we strengthen the *Self* and its influence on us. Our definition of happiness and success, which was dictated by the *Spirit* before we were born and was easy to understand, is now compromised.

Before we were born, we knew the "answers" lay *Within*, in the beliefs of the *Spirit,* where only *Universal Love* was present. There was no conflict, for the *Self* was not present at that time. With our birth, however, and with every subsequent interaction in our life's journey, we learn a new and different set of values and beliefs. With each of these interactions, the *Self* is strengthened as it learns how to survive in the world. The *Self* learns about self-love, happiness, and success, which is defined by our work, prestige, wealth, material possessions, family, friends, and numerous other things we are socialized to believe.

The extent to which we have internalized and believe everything we have been taught will determine how steep the hill we must climb is and how difficult it will be to pass through the *Door* on top of that hill. The stronger our beliefs, the more challenging and difficult the journey will be. For those who have embraced the *"fiction dictated by the Self,"* the hill will indeed be steep and the door difficult to pass through. This fiction is defined as everything we have *"learned"* we *"believe"* will bring us happiness and meaning in our life.

The irony of life is we knew all the "answers," the "Meaning of Life," before we were born, before we were exposed to the harsh challenges of the world, and before we were "taught how to be happy and successful." Though the *Self* is necessary for our daily survival and will accompany us throughout our life, it is also, at least partially, the cause of much of the unhappiness and many of the psychological, emotional, and physical problems and illnesses we experience throughout our lives.

It will be much more difficult to remain on the other side of the door, for those who search for meaning in the world and believe the Self's definition of success and happiness. Even those "lucky" enough to have found "success" and "happiness" in the world, who have a prestigious job, wealth, and many material things, may feel there is still something missing; conflict remains *within* them. This conflict is between the *Self* and *Spirit* and is caused by the difference in their definition as to what success and happiness are. For those who accept and believe what they *"learned"* to be true, the struggle will be harder, the hill steeper, and the *Door* more difficult to pass through. For those who embrace the inherent beliefs of the *Spirit*, however, the answers they seek will come much easier. The hill they must ascend will not be as steep, and the *Door* they must pass through will not be as difficult to approach.

To remain at the top of the hill, to be able to go through the *Door* and not be pulled back through it, *"Acceptance" of the Spirit* must be realized and understood. As we begin to *Awaken*, we may get glimpses of *Enlightenment* as we pass back and forth through the *Door*. It is not until we have fully *accepted* all we have talked about in this book, however, that we finally become "*Enlightened*" and remain there.

Life we see on the other side of the *Door* looks drastically different. Though we are aware the *Self* is still with us, its influence no longer colors many of our actions and decisions. Here, life is looked at through a different prism, primarily through the lens of the *Spirit* rather than the *Self*. The *Light* within each of us, begins to shine brighter, reflecting the calmness and inner peace we now feel. An "aura" of peaceful countenance envelops our body.

On this side of the *Door*, the trivialities and fears we experience in the world during our life become unimportant. The many negative emotions we were taught by the *Self* no longer have much influence on us either. Our lives are now dominated by the *Spirit*. We realize we did *not* give up our individuality and right to live the life we want by *accepting* the views of the *Spirit*, but the exact opposite is true. We discover the life we have always wanted, one where inner peace, love, compassion, and *light*, has come to fruition. We also understand *what we have been taught throughout our lives, our socialization in society, has been the cause of the problems, anxieties, illnesses, and unhappiness* we have felt during our lives and are experienced by many throughout the world.

On this side of the *Door*, when *Enlightenment* becomes a reality, as it was before the *Self* was created, we understand once more that *"Unconditional Love, which is love shared selflessly"* is *"The Meaning of Life."* *We finally understand all life is precious and equal. We also realize and "Accept" almost everything we believed before to be true and important, which we learned in the world, "Was Not".*

Enlightenment is the journey back from the

head to the heart.

~ Ravi Shankar

Chapter 4:

The Mind, Body, Spirit

Connection

Treating the Spirit

The "Spirit" Must be included in the treatment

Of many Psychiatric, Psychosomatic and Medical illnesses.

Treating only the Mental, Emotional or Physical

Part of an illness is not enough.

Medications, Counseling, or any other treatments,

Though quite beneficial, do not Fully treat many illnesses.

Without including the Spiritual contribution to the illness,

The treatment is "Incomplete" and the likelihood

It may return more probable.

Before we discuss the definition of the *Mind, Body, Spirit Connection*, we need to elaborate on exactly what it is. The *Spirit* cannot be discussed using just psychology, which is why we have included a discussion on *Spirituality* to help better understand what the *Spirit* is.

"What is the purpose of the spirit?" It is our belief the *Spirit*, which is *within* every living thing, is an ethereal entity representing *Unconditional Love*, peace, joy, and many other "pure" inherent emotions we identify as positive after we are born. The *Spirit* may be considered to be our *"Higher Self,"* so many of us strive to understand throughout our life. It is often in competition with the *Self* throughout our lives, for the *Self*, unlike the *Spirit,* is only present while we are alive. Many psychiatric, psychosomatic, and medical illnesses are caused by the *Self*. The symptoms of these *Self*-driven illnesses need to be treated

through appropriate accepted treatments, counseling, and medications, if necessary. Currently, treatment, primarily focused on treating just the mind and body, is inadequate. By unifying the *mind, body, spirit connection,* and including the *Spirit* in the overall treatment as well, these illnesses will be treated more *completely.*

Many examples of *Spirituality* and *Enlightenment* can be observed throughout history. One such example is that of the Buddhist monks in the Himalayas. For thousands of years, these monks have known what science is coming to realize: *the Mind, Body and Spirit can be unified and by doing so, result in Enlightenment; further,* the "*Enlightened Spirit*" can accomplish extraordinary feats. These monks are seekers of knowledge who found unity and *Enlightenment* in the training and unification of "*the Conscious Mind, Physical Body, and Spiritual Soul.*"

Many of their abilities derive from the Chinese "*qi,*" which is a form of supernatural energy inherent from one's *Spirit.* Some of these monks have been able to slow their heartbeat, control their body temperature at will, and even manipulate their autonomic body functions, which are generally not under one's conscious control. In the 1980s, Herbert Benson, a Harvard professor of Medicine, observed these monks raise the temperatures of their fingers and toes by as much as 17 degrees and lower their metabolism by 64%.

Another example of such extraordinary abilities is seen in those who practice Reiki, which is a form of alternative medicine developed in Japan in 1922 by Mikao Usui. Reiki practitioners are thought to be able to funnel energy through their hands to heal others. This "*universal energy*" is transferred to another person, aiding in their emotional and physical healing.

Other specific examples of *Enlightenment* can be seen when reviewing the three major world religions that have been practiced for millennia: Christianity, Buddhism, and Islam. *Enlightenment* may be observed through observing the "miracles performed by Jesus, Buddha, and Mohammed." These three prophets appeared to possess magical abilities through the unification of their *Conscious Mind, Physical Body, and Spiritual Soul Connection*. From Jesus healing the sick or walking on water, to Buddha's understanding and use of the six higher knowledges of Iddhi (a paranormal, psychic, or magical power in Buddhism), or Mohammed, whose extraordinary abilities included everything from healing the sick and curing the blind, to his power over nature seen in his call to rain during a drought in Medina, these figures were truly *Enlightened.*

It has been estimated "up to 60 percent of visits to physicians in the United States may be due to stress-related problems, most of which are only partially treated by medication, surgery, or other psychological and medical procedures." It is our belief treatment using techniques involving the *unification of the Mind, Body, Spirit Connection*, will lead to better outcomes for many stress-related illnesses, as well as many other psychological and medical illnesses. Current two-dimensional *Mind, Body* approaches cannot remain as the only treatment; *Spirit* must be involved for a more comprehensive and permanent solution.

By viewing the *Mind, Body, Spirit Connection,* we can look at the world through a different lens. *With the addition of the Spirit, the internal conflict between the Self and Spirit, which often is a contributing factor to the cause of many illnesses, may be fully treated.*

"*We are living in a world dominated by the Self and Fear.*" The result of this is a myriad of conflicts, anxieties, and concerns resulting in the many problems seen in the world today and throughout history. It is a world of hate, anger, jealousy, war, killings, prejudice, hunger, homelessness, illness and so much more. All this is a result of our focus on the *Self*, concerned only for our own self-preservation.

Discussing the *Spirit* causes many, especially those who only accept the views of science, to become uncomfortable. This book is meant to challenge not only them, but also to educate and present a different view of life, one that is long overdue and must be considered.

If we honestly look at what it is like to be living in a world primarily dominated by *Fear and the Self*, then our only conclusion must be life is not only very challenging, but also cruel. Living in a world where the *Spirit* is embraced, however, is quite different. It is a world where the emphasis is on *all* life, in which the *Spirit* is ever-present. Success may only be found when we *all* share and find happiness together. This world of the *Spirit* challenges the views we have been *taught* to believe throughout our lives. In the *Spirit's* world, respect, care, compassion, empathy, and *Unconditional Love* are shared for the benefit of *all*. We accept the *Spirit*, which is present *within* all life, is meant to be shared, and by doing so, the way the world will be viewed will be radically changed forever. The strong, negative, *learned* emotions, which lead to our estrangement from each other, will be muted, as the direction our path takes us on changes.

We are alive to understand and *accept* this truth; this is the lesson we are here to *learn*. This is the *"Meaning of Life"* and is why the *Mind, Body, Spirit Connection* exists. We have a choice to either live in a world of the *Self*, where there is war, hate, and fear, or live in a world where the *Spirit* is *accepted* and its influence is understood, a world where *Unconditional Love*, compassion, and hope exist. We believe it is time to consider the latter.

The understanding of the *Mind, Body, Spirit Connection* can expose new directions and treatments of illnesses, currently treated ineffectively by traditional methodologies, which neglect the *Spiritual* integration into the current two-dimensional mind, body approaches. The relatively new field of Transpersonal *(Spiritual)* Psychology, however, may not be readily accepted within the scientific community. An open mind and *"leap of faith"* will, therefore, be needed, to accept this belief, but the endless possibilities of including the *Spirit* are worth the risk.

In the words of Albert Einstein,

A human being is a part of the whole called by us the universe, a part limited in time and space. He experiences himself, his thoughts, and feelings, as something separated from the rest, a kind of optical delusion of his consciousness. This delusion is a kind of prison for us, restricting us to our personal desires and to affection for a few persons nearest to us. Our task must be to free ourselves from this prison by widening our circle of compassion to embrace all living creatures and the whole of nature in its beauty.

Taoists understand both the mind and the body
are mere tools of the Spirit.

~ Jonathan Lockwood Huie

Chapter 5:

The Spirit Gives Our

Lives Meaning

Do not waste your entire life

Searching throughout the world for

What is already "Within" your Heart.

Though there are very successful combinations of therapy in each

individual field, such as counseling and medications in Psychology, the future may well lie in using a combination of treatments from multiple fields of study. In our case, we are combining the *Mind, Body,* and *Spirit* to format an optimum treatment for each individual person.

Each discipline offers its own unique perspective that together may contribute to a more successful approach. The addition of *Spirituality* allows us to *"accept"* the existence of the *Spirit*. It is our contention the *Spirit* is the missing factor in traditional therapies and must be included to successfully treat many psychiatric, psychosomatic, and medical illnesses. Though partial or temporary improvements may be realized without the addition of the *Spirit*, its inclusion is likely to result in a more permanent, complete, and quicker result. For too long, most treatments focused solely on the *Self (Mind and Body)*. It is time the *Spiritual* side of each person is considered as well.

When only the symptoms of an illness are treated *(Mind and Body)*, the effective sustainable treatment of many psychiatric, psychosomatic, and medical disorders should not be expected. Medication and counseling may prove to be beneficial, but only to an extent. While the *Mind and Body* can be "treated," skills to survive in the world can be taught, and anti-anxiety medication to ease the symptoms of stress can be prescribed, should therapy stop there?

The *Self* is necessary for our survival in the world, though the *"Spirit is as necessary as the Self"* for our emotional, spiritual, and mental well-being. Without the *Spirit*, without striving to "become one" with our *Higher Self*, all that is left is our experiences and survival techniques *learned* since we were born (the *Self*). Though these may help us survive during our life, *without the missing element of the Spirit, our lives will lack meaning.*

When *Spirituality, the "Spiritual Soul,"* is discussed, the emphasis of *Spiritual* has often been on religion; that is not the case here. The *Spirit*, in our definition, has little to do with organized religion. Rather *Spirit* will represent the *"Essence"* (*"Energy"*) within all living things. This includes people, animals, and plants; this energy is even present in the stars and the universe itself.

We will not differentiate between the *Spirit, Essence, Soul, or God*; the differences between each of these four terms will be left up to religious scholars and philosophers to define. For our purposes, the word *"Spirit will be synonymous with the other three.* The *Spirit* is eternal; it is present in utero, during life, and after death. According to some religions, the *Spirit* may return to the Earth via reincarnation to live multiple times, each time, learning lessons and furthering its knowledge about the universal nature of life. Once these lessons have all been learned, the *Spirit* may join others, whose lives also were completed during their last journey, and merge to form one entity in a different realm. To some, this realm is where "*Heaven*" is, and since *God (Spirit)* is present in every living thing, then perhaps *God* is the combination or the totality of all *Spirits* together. There are some philosophers that have theorized every living thing has a small part of *God (Spirit)* within them, and that *God* is the totality of all life together that had once lived and is alive now. This *Essence (God/Spirit)* represents *Unconditional Love* and is what we all strive to return to after we are born.

Those who have been able to *unify their Conscious Mind, Physical Body, and Spiritual Soul* understood and accepted this dynamic between the *Self* and *Spirit,* as well as the importance of *Unifying their Mind, Body, Spirit Connection.* By doing so, they became "*Enlightened.*" This unification significantly decreases the chaos and confusion experienced within each of us. By doing so, it brings the inner peace and meaning we all desire to find in our lifetime. *Each of us can unify our Mind, Body, Spirit Connection as well and become Enlightened.* The goal of this book is to show all how to do this.

"*The Unification of the Conscious Mind, Physical Body, and Spiritual Soul*" has to do with the relationship of the *Mind, Body,* and *Spirit* and the importance of including the *Spirit* in everything we do and all actions we take. The *Spirit* and *Self* often have opposite purposes and their struggle with each other may determine our emotional as well as, at times, our physical health. Our health and emotions often fluctuate according to which of the two are influencing us more at a particular moment. Both the *Spirit* and *Self* are important in our lives, but we suggest both must be considered "*equally*" in every person if there is to be a more permanent solution to the chaotic distress and psychological and medical illnesses often affecting us. If only the *Self* is considered, as is often the case today, the treatment for many illnesses may only be temporary or incomplete. It is our belief the *Spirit* must also be considered, along with the *Self,* for a more permanent long-lasting solution to be realized.

Much has been written already about the *Self (Ego),* so there is no need to further define it here. However, we would like to explore the *Self* in a more *Spiritual* way, rather than just through a psychological prism.

Here, *the Self represents everything we are exposed to and taught to believe is true during our lives, from the moment of our birth, until we die.*

We believe the reason for unresolved depression and for many other illnesses, both psychological and medical, caused by the conflict between the *Self* and the *Spirit*, despite our best efforts using conventional therapy, is that there is a missing third element not addressed: the *Spiritual Soul.* By ignoring this one element in the treatment of many illnesses, only a temporary improvement is often achieved.

By combining our thoughts and focusing our attention on the *Unification of the Conscious Mind, Physical Body, and Spiritual Soul*, we may improve the overall success of traditional therapies which have proven to be unsuccessful on their own. By including the *Spiritual Soul* in the *Mind, Body* equation, a whole new avenue of treatment opens.

We talked about taking a "*Spiritual leap of faith.*" But didn't we take a leap of faith believing Freud when he discussed the *Ego* as well? The *Ego* cannot be seen, heard, or scientifically proven to exist either, yet it has been a pillar of psychiatric dogma for many years. Since we know much about the *Ego*, as it has been discussed at length in many existing papers and books, we will focus primarily on the *Spirit*, rather than the *Ego*, and its effects on our overall health and well-being.

The *Spirit*, as defined in this book, *is the Essence or energy existing within all life*; there is no chaos associated with the *Spirit*. In truth, *Enlightenment is the acceptance of the Spirit within*. Though the *Spirit* cannot be seen or scientifically proven to exist, its effect on our happiness and health should not be disputed.

Just as we know *the Self helps us survive in the world, "the Spirit helps us find meaning in our lives."* By ignoring the *Spirit*, meaning in our lives must come from the world around us; it is our belief such meaning cannot be found there. A *"Spiritually Enlightened"* person understands and *accepts* this; they have found value in their lives from *within* themselves and from their *Spiritual Soul*, rather than from searching for it elsewhere.

Much of what we do involves treating just the *Self*: the Mind and Body. Though we may help others by doing this, the help often is insufficient, allowing for these or other problems, both emotional and physical, to return. We believe, if the *Spirit* continues to be ignored, treatment will never be fully successful.

Each of us must find a balance between the *Self* and the *Spirit*; they are equally necessary to our survival. Both the *Self* and *Spirit* will be with us throughout our lives and depending on which one is more dominate on a particular day, we may have either a "good" or a "bad" day. A good day is when our *Spirit* or *Higher Self* dominates, allowing us to experience the positive inherent emotions within us. These emotions including *Unconditional Love*, inner peace, happiness, and joy, among others, bringing a calm countenance that radiates both within us and in our interactions with the world. A bad day is when the *Self* dominates, reminding us of the many negative emotions present in the world. These emotions may include anger, fear, hate, worry, and sadness. On these days, uncertainty and confusion are often present that may cause mental anguish, anxiety, and depression.

We believe the *Self* is not only the cause or a contributing factor in many illnesses, but it does so to divert our attention from the *Spirit*. When the *Spirit* tries to assert itself and be recognized, the *Self* often reacts by trying to overcome it. One way it does this is by causing us to be sick, either mentally or physically. If our attention is on the world and on our illness, that is created by the *Self*, then it will not be directed towards the *Spirit*.

This constant interaction between the *Self* and the *Spirit* will continue throughout our lives. Treatment, therefore, must involve *both* in order to be successful. It is not until we include the *Spirit* in all our interventions, we can create a more balanced interaction between the two. To treat just the *Self (Mind and Body)* alone, without addressing the *Spirit,* is ineffective. The *Spirit* should be included in *every* treatment in order to assure the best results to heal the *"whole"* person.

Psychosomatic illnesses, which are physical illnesses caused or made worse by emotional responses, may be treated more effectively by including the *"Spirit"* as well. Some common examples of psychosomatic illnesses are peptic ulcers, irritable bowel syndrome, stomach disorders, migraines, back pain and so on. One of the most common causes of psychosomatic problems is stress. Often a clear medical reason for the illness cannot be identified. The symptoms are real, yet when a medical cause cannot be found, those with these illnesses are sent home with little relief. A sedative may help decrease their symptoms and anxieties to an extent, but this solution is only temporary.

We maintain by *treating the Spirit, along with the Mind and Body*, results would be much more effective, successful, and long lasting.

Though much has been written about all three of these elements individually, there is comparatively very little literature considering treatment using all three in combination. By understanding the importance of the *Connection of the Mind and Body* to the *Spirit* in our overall health and happiness, and by including the *Spirit* in everything we do, this book seeks to do just that.

Most people go through life believing they are the thoughts they are thinking, instead of the essence that is experiencing those thoughts.

~ Unknown

Chapter 6:

The Spirit and

Enlightenment

What is "Enlightenment"?

Once you "Accept" the Spirit, rather than the Ego

As your primary guide,

Fear in your life vanishes,

No longer dictating your life.

Spirit's path is Love,

Unconditionally shared with all.

With this "Acceptance" comes "Enlightenment".

Part 1 – Why is Becoming Enlightened So Difficult?

In the Blink of an Eye

Life is quite unpredictable. One moment,

Everything is going well, you are "Successful",

Reaping the rewards earned by "Doing Everything Right".

This may all change, though, "In the Blink of an Eye".

A sudden death, accident, loss of a job, divorce,

War, Famine, Disease, Effects of Climate Change,

Or any number of other life-changing events

May change the rest of your life forever.

We live in a world where this loss may be catastrophic.

To survive, we each must struggle, often mostly alone,

To survive and find our bearings once more.

Life does "Not" have to be like this.

We have only chosen to "Accept" the Values, Beliefs

And Results we Learned living in an Egocentric world.

There is another solution though if anything happens

To disrupt your or someone's else's life,

Even a stranger you may not know,

Someone who may look different

Or have disparate beliefs than you have.

We can "Help" them, in their time of need,

Without expectation of receiving any reward,

Simply because they are fellow travelers,

On a similar Journey Through Life as ours.

The only thing stopping us from living in such

An Altruistic World is our Belief and "Acceptance"

We are better, more deserving than everyone else.

"We Are Not".

Every life is Equally Important.

To truly Change the World, we each must rise up,

Rejecting our Learned beliefs, Embracing instead

The Selfless Spiritual Beliefs Within each of us, within every life.

Together, as one, we may succeed.

Apart, only failure and continuation of the

Unforgiving status quo will continue.

My message is Urgent.

There is No more time to waste.

For if we do Nothing, the future for our children

And for our planet appears quite bleak.

In the 1940s, a psychologist named Abraham Maslow formulated Maslow's Hierarchy of Needs. He used five broad areas, *"Physiological,"* *"Safety,"* *"Love and Belonging,"* *"Esteem,"* and *"Self-Actualization,"* to describe the order in which our needs must be met before *Awakening* and *Enlightenment* may be realized. Once our physiological needs are met, which are at the bottom, then we may progress to the needs listed directly above it. Maslow's hierarchy is represented as a pyramid with the more basic needs, the needs that must be met first, at the bottom, ranging to the realization and acceptance of our *Higher Self,* which he calls *Self-Actualization*, at the top.

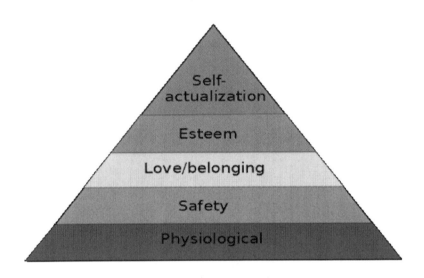

Before we may ascend to the top of this pyramid, our basic needs at the bottom must first be met. Once our *Physiological* needs are met, then we may worry for and consider our *Safety* next. We can then focus on our need for *Love and Belonging*, our desires for *Esteem*, and finally, *Self-Actualization*. If our needs listed under *Self-Actualization* are not first met, then *Awakening* and *Enlightenment* may elude us.

For most of us, many days are tedious; it is a struggle to just survive in the world. We are so focused on our basic needs, we have little time or inclination to consider anything else. Our primary concern is surviving in the world, as we wonder where we are going to live, whether we will have enough food to eat, water to drink, a safe place to sleep, or warm clothing to protect us from the elements. We need to meet these basic *Physiological* needs first before we can even consider anything else.

In our society, the homeless and poor, whose survival and safety are so precarious, their basic needs dominate their every thought and action. For these people, the daily grind of life envelops their entire day. For them, *Self-Actualization* or *Enlightenment* is a distant thought and often, will not even be considered before their basic needs and need for *Safety*, *Love and Belonging* and *Esteem* are met first. It will not be until the bottom four needs on Maslow's hierarchy are achieved, that the final stage of *Self-Actualization* can even be considered.

However, life is never simple and can rarely be explained using just theories or diagrams. The vast majority of us bounce between these levels every day. Some days, we primarily occupy the bottom few rungs of the ladder, worrying only about our survival and safety. On these days, there is little time to consider anything else. On other days though, when our basic needs and safety are taken care of, we may consider other things as well. On those days, meeting our "higher needs" may be possible.

The amount of chaos in our lives often determines which level of the pyramid we occupy on any given day. We may also occupy several levels at the same time. On the days where our life is calm and there are few stressors worrying us, we may spend more time considering our *"Higher Self."* Conversely, on those days where stress and worry dominate our thoughts, most of our time will be spent dealing with our "basic lower needs." Life, though, never proceeds in a straightforward manner. Sources of stress may affect anyone and appear at any time in life. Though we may not have to worry as much about our basic needs if we are wealthy, the concerns in achieving the top three rungs of the ladder still remain. Thus, on a good day, most of our needs are met and there is time to reflect on other things. On a bad day, though, just surviving the day occupies our every waking moment.

Though we may finally reach self-actualization, there are times in our life when we are drawn back to the realities of life. We pass back through the *Door,* falling down the hill, and descend Maslow's hierarchy. Events that cause this to happen are called "*triggers*." A trigger is a memory from earlier in life that returns due to a specific event. This memory is reactivated and returns our emotions and responses to when the memory was formed. Even if we are an adult and this memory was formed when we were much younger, the response we have to this trigger may drag us back to the realities of living in that world, to how we were feeling when the event first happened.

We all have triggers that are activated throughout our life. These may take place anytime and can be caused by even the smallest of events. They are often minor and only cause temporary problems, causing us to fall only partway down the hill, but they still cause us to struggle with the egoistic responses we learned earlier in life. However, there are also major triggers that not only pull us back through the *Door but* cause us to fall to the bottom of the hill as well. When these occur, our life is once again dominated by the *Self,* and we must start our ascension up the hill once more.

Though it may not take as long to climb the hill this time, it still causes us feelings of anxiety and stress that may last a considerable amount of time. All these events cause us to pass in and out of

Enlightenment, as we go back and forth through the *Door* at the top of the hill. Triggers can be fleeting, very short in duration, but they also can trigger major depression and anxiety in our lives and may last for many years.

An example of such a trigger in my life was when my youngest child was 16 years old. My wife, son, and I decided to take a vacation to the west coast of the United States. We drove to Oregon and took the coast highway to Southern California, stopping in many places along the way. Before we left for this vacation, I had asked my wife to be sure to take an extra bottle of aspirin with us, since when I was with my son for an extended period of time, he would often stress me out and give me a headache.

The stress and headaches were caused by him "triggering" my memories from earlier in life. When this happened, I was pulled back through the *Door* and the stress gave me a headache. The stressors were often small, but the triggers were real and caused many physical symptoms. These symptoms were caused by memories I had from years earlier being triggered. Some of these memories were of him growing up, but there were other memories that were reactivated from when I was a little child as well.

I could be fine one moment and the next I was struggling, often returning to the moment and my responses to them when the memory was first formed. Not only would the stress increase my anxiety, but it would also trigger the many headaches I would have when I was with my son. Though we "survived" the vacation and had a very good time, I ended up emptying almost a third of that bottle of aspirin during the trip. The funny part of this story is, unbeknownst to me, before we left on vacation, my son also went to my wife and asked her to take an extra bottle of aspirin on the trip for him, for the headaches *I caused him* to have when he was with me.

Triggers can happen at any time and can be caused by almost anything. If we are aware of some of our triggers, we can learn to, at least partially, control them so their effect on us is not as severe. As depicted, triggers may also be subtle and may be caused by another person, event or even something we see in the world around us. These may profoundly affect our lives and can cause anxiety, depression, as well as a host of other illnesses, both emotional and physical. They provide an additional barrier for us to navigate to not only becoming *Enlightened* but to remain there after we have passed through the *Door.*

Occasionally, we may get glimpses of the peaceful countenance we feel after we are able to walk through the *Door.* Unfortunately, these glimpses are often fleeting, as memories triggered by events, that happened to us many years earlier, drag us back to the "reality" of living in a world dominated by the *Self.* As our *Spirit* is strengthened, however, these events begin to have less of an influence on us. *Though the Self is very strong, its profound control on our life does Not have to be debilitating.* Counseling and medication may help expose and control many of the symptoms we may feel as a result of these triggers. Though the underlying symptoms may be treated and controlled by these traditional means, the addition of the *Spirit* as part of the treatment, may not only lessen the symptoms further, but also prevent them from returning in the future.

It is our belief the stronger the *Spirit's* influence is on our life and, conversely, the less influence of the *Self,* the healthier we will be, both emotionally and physically. In a scientific world, that is a radical statement to make. But it is one we feel must be considered in the overall treatment of many illnesses and our emotional well-being; its inclusion can only be beneficial.

In the 1960s, a fictional TV series called *Star Trek,* took place in the year 2264. In this future, there was no hunger, homelessness, or even any need for money. Replicators synthesized food and water on demand and, just as today's 3D printers, anything we wanted could be replicated as well. Humanity was free to pursue our "*Higher Selves,*" since there was no need to worry about our physiological needs. We do not need to wait for the future for this reality to begin. We have the ability to feed the hungry, clothe and house the needy, provide fresh water to the thirsty, and treat most illnesses and many other problems present in the world today "*Now*". This begs the question, "*Why don't we do this?*"

The answer is quite simple and may be described in just one word, the "*Self.*" Fear, hate, greed, prejudice, entitlement, and concern for only oneself are just some of the negative emotions associated with the *Self* and explain the reason for our inaction. Unfortunately, there are many more negative emotions associated with the *Self* that may be included as well. These self-centered emotions, along with everything we have *learned* throughout our lives, dominate our "better angels."

We accept struggle as an irrefutable part of life. War, murder, disease, prejudice, and much more continue to exist and hunger, fear, and death are deemed *"acceptable."* The *Self* convinces us of this truth, and most of us do not question this or feel that there is anything we can do to change it.

We do "Not" and "Cannot" accept this premise. Without the *Self* dictating our actions, we *"Can"* eliminate hunger, homelessness, most illnesses, and other physiological and safety problems present *"today."* We only need the will to do so. We can eliminate the bottom two rungs of Maslow's ladder *"now,"* freeing all of us to pursue our *Spiritual Higher Selves* and to become *Self-Actualized.* By doing this, our species may finally be able to evolve and produce a more caring, loving world; a world where we treat each other with respect, compassion, empathy, and *Unconditional Love,* rather than continuing to live in a world where there is fear, hate, war, starvation, and disease.

Part 2 – Awakening, Acceptance, and Enlightenment

The Ego and the Spirit

Are they opposites, the Ying & Yang "Within" every life?

As one "Awakens", the Ego begins to loosen its hold

On our journey through life and

The Spirit begins to assert its presence.

This continues as we travel further

On the path towards "Enlightenment".

As the Spirit becomes stronger, the Ego lessens its influence

Until we reach a point where the Spirit

Becomes more influential in our Decisions, Actions

And Path than the Ego.

It is at that point, "Enlightenment" truly begins.

Some of what will be discussed in this chapter may have already been briefly mentioned, but its rephrasing will help put other new ideas into a better and more complete perspective.

In life, we do not need to travel, amass material possessions, have a lot of money, or anything else that may be found in the world to find happiness, meaning, love, and peace. Everything we need to know can be found simply by sitting in a comfortable chair at home, quieting our mind (meditating), and "*listening*" to the messages we receive from *within*. The messages we may "*hear*" from our indelible *Spirit* are life-changing and will bring extraordinary changes to our lives.

If we consider everything happening in the world as a play, then perhaps our priorities in life may change. Though the play may be entertaining, its messages are often based on an *Illusion. The "real" lessons in life may only be found within, where the Spirit is.* The more we seek our answers from the world, the more confused, anxious, unhappy, and fearful we may become.

Many illnesses, both psychological and physical, result from the stress of living in a dysfunctional world, thinking what we have been taught or socialized to believe, is real and important; "it is not." The disconnect between what is real and important, the *Spirit*, and what is not, or *learned* from the *Self*, is the cause of many of the problems, stress, and illnesses that have existed throughout the history of the world and are still present today. When we look at the pain and anguish in the faces of those we pass on the street and read about in the news and on the internet, it only makes us more determined to try to get this message out. *The answers we seek enabling us to find inner peace, love and meaning in our life, may "never" be found in the world by looking outside; they may only be found by looking "within", where the Spirit exists.*

From the moment of our birth, the *Light*, which represents the *Spirit*, begins to *dim* as the *Self* is formed. We are then "socialized" and "taught" about the world around us. This socialization influences us and is the reason for much of the distrust, fear, misery, and illnesses present in the world. *To find the answers we seek, to make our life meaningful and to find true happiness, it is important to reevaluate everything we have "learned" and begin to approach life in a different manner.*

Throughout the ages, many have sought, and failed, to find "*Enlightenment.*" It has been a lofty goal of great religious scholars as well as philosophers, yet it has proved very difficult to discover. We would therefore like to try to make *Awakening* and *Enlightenment* more easily understandable, so others may be able to find it in their lifetime as well.

Awakening is understanding the Spirit exists. Enlightenment is not only understanding the Spirit's existence, but also the "acceptance" of the Spirit and its inherent beliefs that is present within every living thing. The reason *acceptance* is highlighted is because, although many have "*Awakened,*" they have not yet fully "*accepted*" this idea. There have been thousands of books written about *Awakening*; yet, unless this knowledge is internalized, understood, and fully *accepted*, *Enlightenment* will remain elusive.

To reach an understanding of *acceptance*, let us briefly review what has already been discussed. The *Self* is created after we are born by the world around us. It is there to teach us how to survive in the world and "find happiness." *The Self, however, provides us with a false narrative.* Its directive is to convince us concern for ourselves must be preeminent over concern for all life and that happiness and meaning in our lives can be found in the world. It tells us the latter may be achieved if we have prestige, money, or fame, among other qualities that are considered successful in the world. It convinces us if we do not embrace its beliefs, we will be surrendering our "*individuality and right to live the life we want*"; the concepts of individuality and control of our life are thoughts created by the *Self*. If we continue to follow the path the *Self* wants us to pursue, *Enlightenment* will elude us.

When we are *Awakened*, we realize more than just the *Self* is present and influencing us; we begin to *understand* the *Spirit* exists as well. What prevents an *Awakened* person from reaching *Enlightenment* is that this knowledge is not fully *accepted*. There is still a belief, fostered by the

Self, that meaning, happiness, and understanding *"can"* come from the outside world; *it cannot*. Many believe the answers to finding these things lie in being wealthy or being with another person. Though they believe the *Spirit* exists, they still strive to find their answers and happiness in the world around them as well.

An *Enlightened* person, however, understands the latter is not true. They, too, believe in the *Spirit*, though they also understand that *"everything happening around us is of little importance."* An *Enlightened* person believes there is a *Spirit* within every living thing and that *all* the answers we seek in life can *"never"* be found anywhere in the materialistic world; the answers may "only" be found *"within, where the Spirit is."* With *Enlightenment*, the *Wall* erected by the *Self* around the *Spirit* has been eliminated and the *Mask* discarded.

By doing this, we too can free our *Spirit* from its confines. It is at this point we become *Enlightened*, as we realize the path the *Self* has led us on throughout our life has been erroneous and that *"everything we have learned from the moment of our birth was not true"*. The *Self* tells us everything we need can be found in the world. If we even *"partially"* believe this, though we may be *Awakened*, *Enlightenment* will remain elusive. The *Spirit*, however, asks us to seek the answers *within*, where they *have always been* and then share this knowledge and love selflessly with all others. It is ironic we spend our entire life searching for this, yet we have always had the answers. We only had to open our hearts, "*listen*" to our *Spirit* and we would have understood this.

In the moment we "completely accept" everything we have been taught by the Self about "success and happiness" throughout our lives is untrue, and the only truth comes from within, where the Spirit is, Enlightenment will finally be found.

Enlightenment is not a change into something

better or more, but a simple recognition of

who we truly already are.

~ Unknown

Chapter 7:

Living in Enlightenment

Who Am I?

Am I the person you see, hear, touch or

I am I something else?

Am I the many roles I have been assigned by society?

A Father, Husband, Son, Daughter, Janitor, President,

Male, Female, White, Black, Asian, Gay, Straight or

Any of the many other designations we are Defined as

By society as we Accept these choices

We Learned to be true and have been given.

Perhaps I am more than this.

I Am Spirit, as Every life is.

Our body is just a shell housing who we "Truly Are".

We are the same, equally experiencing life.

Our appearance, job, education, race, religion, fame, wealth

Or any other apparent difference between us means little.

Who Am I?

I Am You and We Are All One.

Before we discuss what it is like to be *Enlightened*, we need to examine the consequences of *Enlightenment*. Being *Awakened* and *Enlightened* brings their own set of challenges. These challenges mostly have to do with living in an "*Unenlightened World.*" The struggles, negativity, and unhappiness rampant throughout the world often cause *Enlightened Spirits* to withdraw or to seek out and only want to be with others who are like them. This is very unfortunate because, for those of us lucky enough to have passed through the *Door*, sharing this knowledge with others on the other side of the *Door,* is paramount.

Being around others who view life mostly through a negative lens, though, is difficult and discouraging. This lens, created by the *Self,* is often the result of the *Wall* we each erected early on in our lives. Those whose *Walls* are very thick feel their life is unfair and unjust. They struggle every day, seeing only the negative and worse in life. Instead of viewing life as beautiful, they see it as a challenge to prove to others they are better than them. They often seek out those who are negative like them to share their misery. This vicious cycle proliferates and does little to break down the barriers we have erected to protect ourselves.

Living in a negative world often leads to fear, hate, greed, and selfishness, as we struggle with the many challenges life presents us every day. Negative people are only concerned with their own survival and, therefore, are often unable to break through their protective *Wall.* This *Wall* not only protects them and helps them survive in the world, but it also imprisons their *Spirit* within.

For these people, life is indeed quite challenging and hard. Their negativity, as well, keeps many others from wanting to be around them. They become isolated and do not see the possibilities life has to offer.

Only if their *Wall* can be penetrated, may they finally begin to *Awaken*, take off their *Mask,* and climb the hill leading to the *Door* of *Enlightenment*. Until then, they remain imprisoned in the realm of the *Self.*

It is important we do not abandon them, though this is often difficult to do. Their negativity pushes others away, including those who have viewed what life can be like on the other side of the *Door*. Rather than trying to help them, the opposite is often true; we are repelled by them. However, those who understand and *accept* all we have talked about must not abandon them or anyone else. It is imperative *we help each other*, especially those who are struggling, through life.

We must challenge the many lessons we were *taught* by the *Self* and accept the "advice" of our *Spirit*. We realize, when discussing the *Spirit*, due to the lack of scientific evidence, many will be skeptical taking this step. We maintain, though, with the many problems seen around the world, what is happening now is destructive and damaging. It is, therefore, time to consider changing our direction and trying something different.

While we strive to survive, once our basic needs are taken care of, we each look for meaning and happiness in our life. We do this by being with other people, collecting material possessions, and in many other ways. The hardest part of *Enlightenment* is to realize and know what others are searching for, in the world around them, they will *never* find.

For many, the *Wall* the *Self* has erected to protect and help them survive in the world, not only stops them from approaching the *Door*, but also prevents them from climbing very far up the hill. The self-centeredness and negativity many embrace, due to the many challenges and emotions *learned* in the world, prevent most of us from ascending the hill to any extent.

If we seek the *Meaning of Life* and our happiness in the world by accepting the *Self's* definition of why we are alive, the answers so many of us seek will *never* be found. *Prestige, money, and material possessions may bring an "Illusion of Happiness" but is often temporary.*

The saying "money can't buy happiness" is true. Though it most certainly will make our life easier by assuring our basic needs, such as food, clothing, and shelter, are met, it is not until we understand there is "more" to life than this that meaning can be found. *The Meaning of Life can seldom be found in the world or even by being with another person;*

it may only be found with the knowledge of and "acceptance" of the beliefs of the Spirit within and then, it must be shared.

Those of us who have broken down our *Walls*, ripped off our *Masks*, climbed the steep hill leading to the *Door of Enlightenment*, and passed through the doorway know this. It is difficult to watch so many others, especially those closest to us, continue to struggle every day throughout their lives. Those who remain mired on the hill will not find the answers they seek. The daily struggles of life, worrying about paying their bills and trying to be happy, often occupy their every thought. They may turn to look for meaning in others, especially family, but this too is often fleeting.

It is only by "listening" and "embracing" the Spirit, and "sharing" this knowledge with others, that the true "Meaning of Life" will become clear. Withdrawing from society must not be an option for those who understand this. This knowledge, which was clear to us before we were born and will be once more after we die, must be disseminated. The journey we take in life must be collective, not individual. If we only pursue what is best for us, little will change in the world. *Life's journey will only be "successful" if "everyone" succeeds together.*

It is not that happiness and meaning cannot be found in being with others; it can. It is the reason you are with them that will determine whether your life has meaning. If your reasons have to do with *"conditional love," being with others so "you" can be happy*, then what we seek cannot be found. Conditional love is *learned* by the *Self* by observing others, as we are socialized and *taught* about how life must be led. If, however, the reason you are with others is *"Unconditional"*, *love shared without any expectation of receiving anything in return*, then not only have we broken down our *Walls*, tossed off our *Masks* and climbed the steep hill, but we have also been able to pass through the *Door* to *Enlightenment* and remain there as well.

In 1997, Eckhart Tolle penned a book called *The Power of Now: A Guide to Spiritual Enlightenment*. This insightful book stresses the importance of living in the present moment and avoiding the thoughts and pain of the past or future. Tolle may have based this idea on the Buddha's saying, *"Do not dwell in the past, do not dream of the future, concentrate the mind on the present moment."*

Tolle goes on to talk about "the past being nothing more than all present moments that have gone by, and the future being just the collection of present moments waiting to arrive." Since we are unable to change our past or know what the future has in store for us, regret and worry of what has or will happen is unproductive and useless and leads to unnecessary pain and anxiety. This and many other important lessons can be gleaned from the ideas in this book.

For most of us, though the past may hold many good memories of growing up, there are also many challenges we faced. For some, these challenges may not have been as great or significant as others; nonetheless, their memories still affect them to varying degrees and continue to do so for much or all of their lives. The "lessons" we learn from these events often create memories that may occasionally haunt us. These events may have been small and appeared to be insignificant at the time, but they still contributed to thickening our protective *Wall*. However, other events, we may classify as major, often remain with us as we relive the trauma, at times, every day. Living in the past, continuing to be influenced by the pain associated with many of these emotions, causes anxiety and stress that may contribute to different psychological, psychosomatic, and physical illnesses.

Eckhart Tolle's solution to this, is instead of losing ourselves in the worries and anxieties from the past (or the future) that we cannot change, we need to "live in the present." While it may be easy to see only the "now," in reality, the past does have a profound effect on us, and our dreams of the future give us hope our lives may be better one day. By breaking through the barriers erected by our *Wall* and by tempering our hopes for the future, we believe the lessons Eckhart Tolle presents in his book are invaluable. However, to penetrate the *Wall*, rip off our *Mask,* and be able to *Live in the Now*, the *acceptance* of the *Spirit* is essential.

Now that the difficulties of *Enlightenment* have been discussed, it is time to see what living in an *"Enlightened World"* can be like. Fear, jealousy, prejudice, and hate, rampant throughout the world today and throughout history, would no longer be present. They, instead, would be replaced by *Unconditional Love,* empathy, and compassion for all.

No longer would the world be dominated by greed, avarice, and concern only for ourselves. Instead, the *Spirit* would dominate, rather than the *Self,* whose *Self*-ish desires drive many of the world's problems. All the world's resources would be shared equally. There would no longer be hunger, homelessness, or death from treatable illnesses. Money would no longer be the most important commodity, replaced instead by love and concern for *all*.

Everyone would be equal; there no longer would be any castes dividing us. The amount of money we have, material things we own, kinds of jobs we work, the color of our skin, or anything else currently dividing and defining us in society would no longer matter. We would recognize and *accept,* though the *Self* is necessary for our everyday survival in the world, it could no longer dictate our thoughts and actions.

There would no longer be any need for war because all our resources would be equally shared. *Unconditional Love, which is love given without expectations,* would be shared freely and our interactions with each other would become *Spiritually* motivated, rather than primarily motivated by the *Self.*

There would be no loneliness, knowing the *Spirit* is accompanying each of us on our journey through life. Moreover, our *Spirit* would be shared with all others in which a *Spirit* is present as well. Religion would no longer divide us, but rather, the *Spirit* within every living thing, would be universally recognized and unite us. It would no longer matter if we were Catholic, Protestant, Buddhist, Hindu, Muslim, Jewish, or any other religion. All religions would be recognized as equal, with no one religion being better than the other.

Climate change, one of our greatest challenges today, would no longer exist; we would all use resources respecting and safeguarding all life, eliminating global warming. We have the technology *today* or we will have it soon to accomplish this; all we need is the will and desire to do it. *Self*-ishness would be replaced by *Self*-lessness, where concern for everyone's well-being would replace concern for only ourselves.

We do not go through life alone; both our *Self* and *Spirit* accompany us on our journey through life. The *Spirit*, which represents a small piece of the *Essence* (*God*), is present within all living things and connects all life. By sharing our *Spirit* with all other living things, we amplify its power exponentially to improve *all* our lives.

When we communicate with each other, it is done mostly through the eyes of the *Self*, rather than through the connectivity of the *Spirit*. As such, there are often ulterior motives involved, resulting from what we have *learned* throughout our life and what we hope to gain for ourselves through our interaction. This often results in us trying to convince someone to do or believe something. *Our communications are therefore mostly superficial, dictated by our needs, beliefs, and desires ingrained in us by society as grow up.*

There is another way, however, to relate to others: the way of the *Spirit*. Instead of relating to another as a result of our *Self*-ish needs, *Spirits* communicate with each other in an entirely different way, one driven by *Selflessness* and compassion. There are no ulterior motives as one *Spirit* interacts with another. Rather, *Spirits* interact on a higher plane with no expectations of benefit for themselves.

There is no need to wait until we are no longer alive to be able to communicate with others in this way; it is possible to share this pure bond now. Interacting like this means our *Spirit* directly connects to the *Spirit* within another, without the interference or addressing the needs of the *Self*.

To *Awaken* and become *Enlightened* is just the beginning of our journey. To be able to directly peer into the *Soul* (*Spirit*) of another is extraordinary and has not been experienced by many, though it is possible. It is the next logical step in the *Spiritual* growth and evolution of humanity. This is the purest form of communication that may be experienced during one's lifetime. To learn to communicate with another on a purely *Spiritual* level is a lofty goal and will bring unsurmountable inner peace to those who come to understand, *accept,* and live their life this way.

We all too often judge others by their appearance, actions, and other factors influenced by society and our upbringing. To be able to "see" someone, not as a product of who they appear to be, but rather as a pure *Spirit,* is how we are truly meant to interact with each other. Instead of trying to convince or judge someone by what we hope to get from them, we are meant to connect with each other on a much different higher existential and unpretentious level.

Imagine a world where our children, who are currently socialized to believe the "teachings" of the *Self,* are raised instead to understand the *Spirit within* them. They would be brought up knowing compassion, empathy, and the need for and importance of treating everyone equally. No longer would we ignore the suffering of others, but rather, we would help those in need who are struggling through life's challenges.

Our children would now be raised in a world dominated by the *Spirit* rather than the *Self.* Here, material things and self-concern would be replaced by the understanding that everything must be shared and every person, every *Spirit,* is equally important. They would be raised and "socialized" to know *the "Meaning of Life" can only be found by "listening" to the Spirit, and by sharing and helping others, their lives will be meaningful and important.* They would realize to be truly happy in life, they must search *within, accept the guidance of their Spirit,* and care equally about *all* life. They would also understand they will *never* find true happiness or meaning from the many distractions found in the world around them.

In the 1960s and 70s, there was a movement embracing many of these values. "Hippie" Communes, where adults and children lived together, shared everything and their concern for each other replaced the struggles of living in an individualistic, competitive world. In such communes, all resources were shared, and all the children were brought up by the collective, rather than by individual parents. The children were raised knowing and understanding the value of sharing, love, and compassion. There was cooperation between everyone; no one was without shelter, hungry, or alone. Food was grown collectively with everyone equally sharing the bounties of the earth. Decisions would be made by the collective, considering what was best for all, rather than just the individual. The sway and importance of money and other material things meant little here; those who had more would share their excess with others. No one was considered better than another; the color of their skin, age, sex, beliefs, or anything else did not matter.

Around the same time in history, the rise of the civil rights movement took place. One of the great leaders of this movement was Martin Luther King Jr. One of the most important messages of love he spread came from a speech he gave in Washington, D.C., in 1963. Among the most quoted lines of this speech are *"I have a dream that my four little children will one day live in a nation where they will not be judged by the color of their skin, but by the content of their character."* The inclusion of *Enlightenment,* in this speech, would simply change the end of his statement to *"the content of their Spirit."*

The *Spirit*, which is often hidden behind the *Wall* we erect as children to protect ourselves from pain and events of the world, would no longer be imprisoned or influenced by outside forces. It would be freed, and *the content of each Spirit* would be equally shared with everyone. The Love, compassion, and empathy of the *Spirit* would be given and shared without expectations.

The result of releasing the *"content of our Spirit"* would be staggering and monumental. There would be a shift, an evolution, where we would finally embrace the teachings of the *Spirit*, rather than those of the *Self*. In an ideal world, this Darwinian evolution would eliminate and make extinct those who believe the content of their *Self* defines their existence, rather than the content of their *Spirit*.

The journey of life will only have meaning if "everyone" succeeds. We *all* must help each other break down our *Walls*, rip off our *Masks*, ascend the hill and pass through the *Door* to *Enlightenment*. There will be times when we need help breaking through the *Wall* or pushing each other to the top of the hill; we therefore must always be there to help each other.

Success, happiness, and meaning can only be found if we *all* "work together" to assure our mutual happiness and success; it may never be found in the world being concerned only for ourselves or following the directives of the *Self*. Those of us who have conquered the *Wall*, the *Mask,* the *Hill,* and the *Door* must never withdraw from society or just be with only those who are like us. Rather, we must help everyone else, who are still struggling with their *Self*-ish obstacles, so they too may find meaning in their lives as well.

It is possible to live life this way, but it will take a radical change for it to occur. It will take a redirection of belief in what is possible and a *"leap of faith"* to pursue a new uncharted path for our future. Instead of *accepting* and choosing to live in *Fear* we must instead choose to live with *Love*.

He who knows others is wise;

He who knows himself is enlightened.

There are many paths to enlightenment.

Be sure to take the one with a heart.

~ Lao Tzu

Chapter 8:

Choosing Love over Fear

Fear vs Love (Ego vs Spirit)

As we were growing up, we were "Taught" how to act,

What to Believe and how to Survive in the world (Ego).

If we accepted what we had Learned, as the great majority of the world has,

We were Taught to be primarily concerned about Ourselves,

"Our" happiness and Our survival in the world.

We were told if we made a lot of money, we will be successful and happy.

By accepting this Learned view of the world,

We also Learned to live our lives in "Fear".

And with Fear, comes many other negative emotions seen

Throughout our very polarized world.

Imagine, instead, growing up where there was concern for "Everyone",

Rather than for only Ourselves (Spirit).

Success and happiness would only happen if "Everyone" succeeded in life.

By accepting this Inherent view of the world, we would live our lives

with "Love".

The love I am talking about is not what we learn or read about,

"Conditional" love, which is given with the expectation we will get

love back.

Rather, this "Unconditional" love comes from within

And is given without reservation.

For our children and the world to flourish,

We must reverse the paradigm of life and

Choose "Love" over "Fear" (Spirit over Ego).

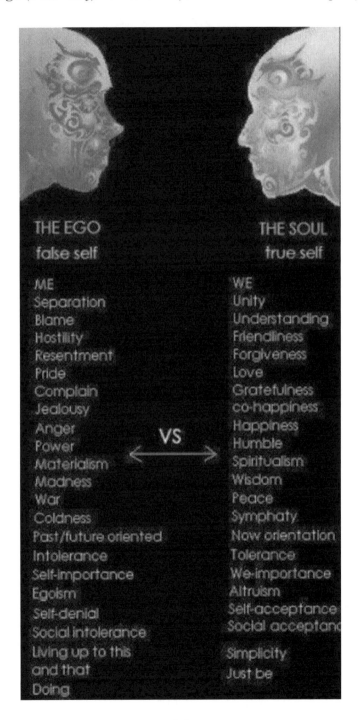

There are two predominant emotions we may choose between throughout our life: *"Love"* and *"Fear."* *Love* (*Soul* or *Spirit*) represents all that is good in our lives and includes compassion, empathy, care, joy, serenity, hope, gratitude, contentment, kindness, inspiration, and all other *inherent* positive traits and emotions. *Love* originates from the *Spirit* and is what gives our life meaning. To experience and share this *Love* with others, where *Spirit* is present as well, is why we are born; it is the *"Meaning of Life."* This is the lesson we are here to learn, yet there are many obstacles placed in our way that may alter our path.

These obstacles may be described in one word: *"Fear"* (*Ego* or *Self*). *Fear* is what prevents us from learning these lessons and includes hatred, anger, worry, stress, loneliness, sadness, jealousy, envy, shame, prejudice, and all other *learned* traits and emotions largely considered negative in society.

These negative emotions are *learned* by the *Self* throughout our lives and are what prevent us from finding the inner peace and happiness we all so desperately seek. They are also, at least partially, the cause of illness, struggle, depression, and misery seen in the world today and throughout history.

After we are born, everything we see, hear, and learn affects our view of the world. We are *"taught"* how to survive in the world, but we also *learn* from observing others and all the interactions we are part of throughout our lifetime. We *learn* how we should treat each other and what happiness is. We also learn everything we need to know from our parents, friends, movies, books, the internet, religion, and many other venues. They *teach* us what *"success and happiness"* are. The result of this is often anxiety, confusion, and other negative emotions and illnesses previously mentioned. We believe we will be successful and find happiness if we are wealthy, so we may experience and buy the "best things" in life. But even if we are granted our wish and become rich, we may find the happiness we seek continues to elude us.

We are all equal because we all have a *Spirit* within us. The color of our skin, gender, sexual orientation, weight, height, wealth, role in society, or any other comparison we would like to make matters very little; there is no real difference between us. All these comparisons and differences have one thing in common: they are created by the world around us, by the *Self*. It is easy to get confused and accept these comparisons as reality, which allow for something very valuable to become lost. By accepting the *Self* as our predominant guide in life, the

Light within, our *Spirit*, dims.

Most of us struggle to survive in the world, pay our bills, take care of our family, and deal with the harsh reality's life presents us. Many of us have had challenging childhoods, which include heavy baggage we must deal with and carry for the rest of our lives. Every interaction we have, after we are born and until our death, affects us and how we will react to the world. *Fear,* anger, hate, sadness, and other negative emotions are formed and may remain with us, as we are growing up and exposed to the many difficulties life present each of us.

Even though we also have positive emotions, like *Love,* caring, and compassion, many of these are "conditional"; they are "*pseudo emotions*" created by the *Self,* rather than the *Spirit. Pseudo emotions are emotions that are learned; these emotions* try to convince us we are leading a happy, content life. The reality, though, is often these "*Learned*" emotions simply distract and convince us we are on the right path, the path the *Self* has chosen, rather than the path the *Spirit* has prescribed for us.

It is interesting how different each of our paths are, how every person finds their own path and how everything we have been exposed to while we are alive helps determine the path we will take. Every one of us have struggles we must deal with. For some, these struggles may be easier than for others, though no one goes through life unscathed.

Our views of the world are reformed every day and may be unduly influenced by a single event as well. Whether that event is a tragedy, such as the death of a loved one, or something else, we find our lives are forever changed as a result. For others, there are events in life taking place every day that may affect them throughout their lifetime. For example, there are some children who grow up seeing and experiencing untold horrors. To them, watching others die from war or starvation is common and part of their everyday reality. They appear to go through life in a daze, simply trying to understand and survive the many different challenges life presents to them every day.

We live in a world where *Fear* rules many of our thoughts and actions. Besides all we have talked about, we also have the *Fear* of living and dying as well. The *Fear* of living is understandable for we live in a very combustible and uncertain world where our survival may be challenged every day. There are places in the world where even children who are walking to school are in danger. Besides our concerns for our safety, we worry and are afraid our basic needs will not be met.

There is also intense hate and anger present throughout the world. There is a helplessness permeating our *Spirit*, as we feel unable to do anything to change the future. There always appears to be a war somewhere in the world, or hunger, disease, extreme poverty, and many other challenges to life due to the greed and avarice of humanity.

Unfortunately, we persist in finding new ways to create *Fear* in the world. We have devised many ways to kill each other, including guns, bombs, knives, and many other ingenious ways. If we were to examine some of the wars closer, it just does not make sense. Many of them have been fought over religion. We see Jews curtailing Muslims rights, Hindus persecuting Muslims, Catholics being pitted against Protestants, Shiite Muslims shunning Sunni Muslims, just to mention a few. Even though people in each of these groups may look like each other, the only difference is their beliefs in *God.*

We also see fear and hate if someone looks or acts differently. Whether this difference is skin color, gender, or sexual orientation, we have the need to feel superior to those who are different. Therefore, we treat others without the respect every person deserves. For example, Neo

Nazis and other right-wing ideological groups feel the white race is better than all others and anyone who does not look or believe like them is simply inferior and sub-human.

The similarities between all these groups show how pervasive hate and *Fear* have been throughout time. These examples above do not reflect all the reasons for such intense *Fear* and hatred toward others. All hatred is "*learned*"; we are not born with "hate in our hearts." What we *learn* in society and our experiences during our life often result in these actions and "beliefs."

It is extraordinary such prejudices exist in life or there can be such hatred. *Fear is learned; it all* is the result of the *Self.* We are born knowing none of this. We spend our entire lives simply trying to return to this moment, one before we were born, when life "*made sense.*" *The Meaning of Life*, the goal of our existence, the reason we are alive, is to understand this and by doing so, open our hearts once more to the inherent compassion and *Unconditional Love* within every person. There is *never* a sufficient reason for war, to feel superior to others, or our inhumanity towards each other. If we continue to believe there is and continue to follow the course humanity has followed from the onset, then our survival may be in peril.

Poverty and starvation, caused by the uneven distribution of our resources, are seen in many parts of the world and are two of the many causes of misery and *Fear* in the world today. Nelson Mandela, a South African anti-apartheid activist and political leader, among the many issues he addressed, talked about the effects of "*The Prison of Poverty*" on society. He described how "massive poverty and obscene inequality are such terrible scourges of our times, times in which the world boasts incredible advances in science, technology, industry and wealth accumulation; poverty and hunger are not natural. They are man-made and can be overcome and eradicated by the actions of human beings." We have the ability "*now*" to dramatically improve the lives of those in poverty and get rid of the *Fears* associated with it; all we lack is the will and *Spiritual* compassion to do so.

Many thousands each year also die from the effects of climate change on our environment. Hurricanes, tornadoes, earthquakes, tsunamis, flooding, drought, raging fires, and more are made worse by global warming and are destroying our planet and causing untold loss throughout the world. By the year 2100, catastrophic global warming is expected as temperatures are projected to rise by an average of 4 degrees. The last time the Earth was as warm, its oceans were hundreds of feet higher. The resulting flooding and death will be extraordinary. And if all of this is not bad enough, we also *Fear* death and the unknown.

There is so much *Fear* in the world, and with this *Fear* comes many negative emotions. The effects of these emotions and feelings are devastating, as we try to survive in a *Self*-ish world devoid of the *Spirit's* love. *Living in constant Fear prevents us from releasing our Spirit's potential and imprisons us in a world where Fear dominates our lives every day.* If *Fear* is our primary emotion, *Love* will be secondary, giving way to the aforementioned vicious cycle destined to repeat itself in perpetuity. It is only by realizing the insanity of this change may be possible; and it is only by treating each other with respect, compassion, and *Unconditional Love*, may we all finally evolve to a higher plane of existence.

There are many choices and paths we may take in life. The choices we make are often determined by whether we choose to live our life with *"Love or Fear"*. *If we choose to live with Love, then the "Illusions" of the Self must be* confronted. The realization, understanding and *"acceptance"* that money, or many of the other things we *learn*, or were *taught* as we were growing up, will *not* bring meaning or true happiness in our lives. Though we have *"succeeded"* in life, followed all the rules and what we were taught from the moment of our birth and have enough money to live well, we still find ourselves looking for meaning and happiness. *This happiness is "conditional"; it is the result of being "successful" in the world. We are living an "Illusion of Happiness."*

Which of these two paths we choose, *"Love or Fear,"* will also determine many of the challenges we face in life. If we follow the path of *Fear*, the path the *Self* has charted for us, these challenges may be difficult and may result in many emotional and physical illnesses as well as unhappiness, stress, anxiety, depression, and struggle. If, however, *Love* is chosen, then many of these problems will not present themselves.

The love we refer to here is *"Unconditional Love,"* not the romantic love often written about in books or seen in movies. This love comes from the *Spirit,* is selfless and given without expectations. It allows us to experience many of the positive inherent emotions previously described, and by sharing these emotions with others, our lives become meaningful.

Romantic love, however, is *"conditional"* and given with the expectation we will benefit from sharing it with someone else. This is the love we *learn* about as we are socialized and taught about life. We look for this love from others and, though we may believe we have found it, it is often just an *"illusion."* *Conditional Love* will *never* bring the happiness or meaning we seek in our lives. We think it will since this is what we were *taught; it will not.*

The many stressors and chaos we experience throughout our lives often cloud our judgement and actions. Even if we followed what we believed to be true and were taught throughout our lives, it often does not lessen the internal struggles so many of us face daily. We may have "found" love and yet we know, deep within, there is still something missing. We have not come to the realization and understanding yet that *"love that is learned, conditional and found in the world, is often fleeting and temporary."*

Unconditional Love, however, is not temporary. It is present within each of us, though often unable to shine its *Light* brightly due to the darkness present in the world. For some, who have accepted much of what we were *taught* throughout our lives, the *Light* is barely visible. For others, however, who begin to question and "sense" there is more, whose

Wall starts to crack and begin to "*Awaken,*" the *Light* may begin to shine a little brighter.

We start to realize what we have been taught and socialized to believe, will not bring us the inner peace, happiness, and love we so desperately hope for. We begin to understand what we thought and were taught would bring us these feelings, *will not.* We sense a "*voice*" *within*; though we may have heard it before, it is now more prominent. As we begin to "*listen*" to this voice, we start to understand *the peace, happiness, and love we have sought throughout our lives was always there; "we were only looking for it in the wrong place."*

When we become *Enlightened,* this finally becomes clear. To truly change the trajectory the world is on now, this message must be shared so others may realize it as well. There is no longer room for *Fear* in the world; there is only room for *Love.* Each of us must decide our own path. It is our hope we choose that path wisely, "*Choosing Love Over Fear*".

One of the characteristics of an *Enlightened* person is *humility.* With *Enlightenment*, there is no need for fame, recognition, prestige, money, or any such accolade of the world. Such traits are treasured by the *Self* and its need for acceptance and importance. In reality though, an

Enlightened person knows and *accepts* we are all equal and no one is better than another, regardless of their accomplishments in the world. There is no need or desire to speak poorly about someone else or complain about life being unfair to prove we are superior to others. We all have our individual journey we must pursue, though *all of our journeys are connected.* If we are to succeed, *everyone* must be successful as well. There is no competition between *Spirits*, rather *Unconditional Love* and a desire for *all* to be successful in their journey through life.

An *Enlightened* person views success in a different way while they are alive. To them, though the *Self* continues to help them "survive" in the world, they come to this realization much earlier in their life. They understand and view life through a *Spirit*ual lens, rather than the predominant lens of the *Self.* As such, success to an *Enlightened* person is understanding everything a dying person does but much earlier in their life and *sharing* this knowledge and *Unconditional Love* with others so *everyone* may succeed in their journey through life.

One of the reasons we are writing this book is to share this knowledge with you. It is our hope, by sharing this, many more will

Awaken and become *Enlightened.* Only by sharing and helping each other, will inner peace, meaning, and true happiness finally be able to spread throughout the world. And by doing this, the trajectory of life may be changed, assuring the future survival and happiness of our children.

There are two basic motivating forces: fear and love.

When we are afraid, we pull back from life.

When we are in love, we open to all that life has to offer with passion, excitement, and acceptance.

We need to learn to love ourselves first, in all our glory and our imperfections. If we cannot love ourselves, we cannot fully open to our ability to love others or our potential to create.

Evolution and all hopes for a better world rest in the fearlessness and open-hearted vision of people who embrace life.

~ John Lennon

Chapter 9:

Living with Spirit in

Your Life

The Spiritual Path

Enlightenment is a journey, often long, challenging, and lonely,

Many "Have No Choice" but to follow.

Despite how "Successful" our life may be,

There is a feeling deep "Within", something is wrong;

A feeling that simply will not abate.

This "Awakening", will lead to disavowing "Everything"

We have "Learned" and "Accepted" as True during our lifetime.

Beginning us on a Spiritual Path of Self-Discovery.

We have talked about *Spirit, Awakening and Enlightenment*, but the next question is: *what's next*? Once the existence of the *Spirit* is realized and *accepted*, *sharing* this knowledge is the next logical step. In a world, where *fear*, hate, prejudice, and many other negative *learned* emotions are present, our evolution and survival depend on *sharing* this "message" with everyone.

When I was in high school, I went with my friends to an amazing music festival called Woodstock. I remember I was 17 years old, sitting around a fire in a light rain. A bottle of wine and a pipe filled with marijuana were being passed around the fire, and, of course, extraordinary music was playing in the background. It was at this point in my life I became a *"hippie"*; perhaps the hippies had it right after all. I thought this was the greatest culture of all time. This culture was designed to *share the Unconditional Love* of the *Spirit*; the hippies knew this was the path that should be taken.

Unfortunately, the *Self* has a way of creeping back into our life. As this generation got older, many of them fell back "in step" with what they were *taught* by the *Self* as they were growing up. The harsh realities of life caught up with them and the *Self* reasserted its control and dominance. Many of the hippies, as did members of all other generations, ended up getting married, having children, getting jobs, buying a house, paying bills, and dealing with the everyday difficulties and stresses life presents each of us.

The hippies began to change; their path, once dictated by the *Spirit*, now was once again dominated by the *Self*. The *Unconditional Love* they shared with "everyone" soon became more *Self*-centered. They learned they needed to take care of themselves and their families. They got caught up thinking they would find happiness if they got married, had a lot of money, and collected material possessions. They forgot about *Unconditional Love* and focused on *Self*-love instead. Society won with this generation, as it did with so many other generations.

The hippies realized the *Self* brought unhappiness and were convinced the answers lay elsewhere. However, much like my contemporaries, I am also guilty of abandoning my path. Though I very much enjoyed my weekend with the hippies at Woodstock, when I returned home, the realities of life presented themselves to me once again. My focus returned to being *"successful"* in life, or at least to what I thought being successful meant at that time.

The *Journey to Enlightenment* is not only very difficult, but also very lonely. Almost all our family, friends and acquaintances are so wrapped up in their daily struggles and following what they were *taught* will bring them happiness, they have little time or inclination to think about anything else. Though they may see occasional glimpses and wonder whether there is something more, they do not pursue this. Often, our spouses and others we deeply care about, live a life dictated by the *Self;* when they think of *Spirit,* it is mostly in a religious, rather than *Spiritual,* sense. Though religion is important to many, our focus in this book has little to do with organized religion. To us, *Spirituality* is more personal and has to do with first *Awakening* and then seeking to become *Enlightened* by understanding and *accepting* the *Spirit* within.

As we search for answers and begin to *Awaken,* we read "spiritual" books and meditate, trying to understand if there is more to life than just what the *Self* has taught us. In our "gut," we know there is, and though we still may get caught up in the daily struggle's life presents us, we continue to try to understand what it is we are feeling.

In a religious sense, this journey may take many lifetimes; this is the Hindu belief of reincarnation. In a *Spiritual* sense, though, this may begin to occur just before we die, when the *Self* has less sway over our thoughts. For those lucky enough, who have been able to internalize the message of the *Spirit* earlier in their lives, their life will *never* be the same.

With Awakening and Enlightenment comes internal peace, Unconditional Love, and true happiness. The happiness we are talking about has little to do with what we were *taught* will make us happy. When we become *Enlightened*, we understand true happiness can never come from anywhere but *within*, where the *Spirit* is, and only by *sharing* that *Love Selflessly* with all others will our life be meaningful. When we *"accept"* this truth, our lives will be changed forever. At that point, we realize what we thought was important, *was not,* and the happiness we found from everything we were *taught* about growing up was simply an *"Illusion of Happiness."*

Living in an unenlightened world can also be very challenging.

Observing the fear, hatred, killing, war, starvation, homelessness, illness, and more is heart breaking, for we know these things are preventable. They are a result of living in a world dominated by *Fear* from the *Self*, rather than *Love* from the *Spirit*.

On a more personal level, watching those we love and care about struggle is very difficult as well. Our spouses, children, parents, siblings, and friends may be starting to *Awaken*, but often are not. Unless we actively seek out and only associate with others seeking *Enlightenment* as well, we find we are mostly alone. Those of us who have become *Enlightened* are often viewed as strange and eccentric. Though we initially try to share our knowledge, we often do not talk about it very much with those we care about and love; they are often so entrenched in their *learned* beliefs, they have little interest in what we are trying to tell them.

We do have an obligation, though, to do something positive and share this knowledge with others. *Enlightenment* is a gift; those lucky enough to have achieved it in their lifetime must share it. To change the world, we must work to alleviate many of the fears and hatred that exist today.

Success, to an *Enlightened* person, exists only when *"everyone"* is successful, not just yourself; *only then will life have meaning.* This journey through life is to understand and *share* this knowledge with each other, as well as to selflessly help *everyone* succeed.

As a species, we have a very harsh reality that must be confronted; we must either *evolve* or become *extinct.* Just as Darwin discussed in *The Theory of Biological Evolution,* we introduce here a new theory, which we will call *The Theory of Spiritual Evolution.*

The Theory of Spiritual Evolution involves the *Awakening, Acceptance, Enlightenment, Sharing, and importance of the Spirit* to help promote a better world. One of the reasons for this book is to *share* the Spirit's wisdom in our everyday lives. This is true, especially for the children of the world. Our *evolution* depends on the generations to come internalizing and sharing this message, and by doing so, changing the direction the world is going in.

Unlike the hippies, this generation must not only *Awaken* and become *Enlightened,* but they must also not revert to believing the false promises of the *Self.* The *Spiritual Evolution of our Species* will only take place when these beliefs not only thrive but spread further to their children and beyond. As this happens, hopefully, as Darwin hypothesized, those who practice only *Self*-love and *Self*-preservation, will hopefully dwindle, becoming extinct. The resulting world will be one where we care for each other and where *Unconditional Love* and compassion exist and are *Self*lessly shared.

With the many problems in the world, if this evolution does not become a reality, then extinction is a very real possibility. When society is dominated by *Fear* and the *Self*, rather than *Love* and the *Spirit*, we must ask: how is extinction not the obvious result?

Throughout recorded history, from the beginning of time, there has been war. War is a product of many things, but we would like to focus on just one of the main causes – the *Self*. Some of the traits of the *Self* we are *taught* and *learn* about in our lifetime make it easy for us to kill each other; these traits include *Fear*, greed, hatred, prejudice, and other negative *learned* emotions.

In an *Enlightened* world, there would be no war. There would be no fear, hate, greed, or prejudice; everything would be equally shared. In this idealistic society, one where the lies of the *Self*-ish world have been exposed and our lives are primarily dominated by the *Spirit*, there is only peace. It is a world where all life is respected and treated as equal, a world where we help and share with each other to assure our mutual happiness and survival. There is no need to kill someone for food, shelter, or any other reason; instead, everything is shared equally.

We have the technology *today* to accomplish this. We can eliminate many of the reasons that cause war, such as ensuring everyone's basic needs and safety are met. If our resources were more equally divided, there would be no hunger, for food would be plentiful and clean water, housing, clothing, and medicine could easily be provided to every person in need as well. Yet, there are many in our society dying every day of starvation, curable diseases, and other preventable illnesses. How does a civilized society watch and allow any child or person die of starvation, thirst, or a curable disease?

If this shift were to occur, many of the reasons for war would no longer exist; the greed, fear, avarice, prejudice, and hatred of the few, who "convince" the rest of the need to kill "their enemies", would hold little sway. When I was growing up, the Vietnam War was ongoing. During this war, hundreds of thousands of people died on both sides because of the greed of a handful. Though we were lied to and told many reasons we had to fight, the real reason was that Vietnam had valuable resources that some in America wanted to exploit. This war, as with all wars, was fought due to the greed and desire of the select few to become wealthier.

Everyone who died during the war, and during all other wars, perished for no reason. The pain, anguish, debilitating injuries, and countless deaths were for what? It is our contention, in an *Enlightened* world, where resources are shared fairly and greed and hatred lose their hold on society, there would not be a reason for war. There also would be no reason for *Fear*.

We are here, in our brief journey through life, to learn. We maintain what we are here to learn about is *sharing Unconditional Love,* selflessness, empathy, and compassion, rather than *fear*, greed, and hatred. *Self*lessness is helping each other *unconditionally*, without expectation. Those who are *Enlightened* understand this; those who are not, accept the realities of death, hunger, homelessness, and other daily struggles our fellow travelers are exposed to every day, as unfortunate, but unavoidable.

Though this book will not discuss *Spirituality* in a religious manner, it is important to address organized religion at least briefly, since it affects such a large portion of general society. There are many religions and beliefs in the world. Many of these religions, though different, have similar characteristics. Rather than delve into each individual religion and the differences in their beliefs, we will focus on how religion has been used to justify killing and other atrocities throughout history.

Whether someone is Catholic or Protestant (Northern Ireland), Christian or Muslim (the Crusades), Jewish or Muslim (the Middle East), Hindu or Muslim (India and Pakistan), or any of the other dualities in contrast, religion has been the reason for many wars as well as much killing, hatred, and *Fear* throughout time. The reasons given for the wars mainly have to do with the many fallacies, *Fears,* and the hatred instilled in society by others through our *Self*-ish beliefs.

Religion, rather than uniting us, often divides us instead. Religious leaders talk about God, love, compassion, and caring for each other, yet those who follow their teachings rarely internalize these lessons. Instead, they are taught and socialized to believe these teachings have to do with the world around them, rather than from the *Spirit* within. The emotions taught by religions are often *pseudo-emotions*, which are *"learned"*, rather than the pure, *inherent unconditional* emotions advocated by the

Spirit.

Spirituality has a different view to that of religion. *Spirituality* concentrates its beliefs on our *inherent emotions,* that exist *within* each life, *not* on our *learned pseudo-emotions.* We understand *success in life can only be accomplished by everyone succeeding together and not by our individual accomplishments.* By improving ourselves and sharing the pure inherent beliefs of *Spirituality and Enlightenment,* with others, there would no longer be a need for war, hatred, greed, or *fear.*

Though organized religion's original goal was to help, its message and purpose slowly became obscured by the "teachings" of the *Self,* which replaced the original altruistic message of the *Spirit.* The frailties and temptations of the world interfered with the messages they were trying to teach. As a result, the opposite of what they had hoped for came to fruition.

It is our contention, only by changing oneself from *within,* by accepting the beliefs of *Spirituality,* and by sharing this with others, can *Enlightenment,* which so many of us strive to reach, be found and real change take place. *"Real change must be found within each of us first and then shared selflessly with the world."*

Imagine the beauty of living in a world where peace and love are everywhere. In the early 1970s, John Lennon, a prolific songwriter, penned an extraordinary song called *Imagine*. The song invites its listeners to imagine what the future could be like if only we followed Lennon's dreams. In the song, he asks "What if there is nothing to divide us; if there is no Heaven or Hell, no countries or war, no religion or possessions, or greed or hunger." He ends his song singing about "living in peace, (among) a brotherhood of man and of sharing the world, so that the world will live as one." It is a song about universal peace and *Unconditional Love,* and if you get a chance, we hope you will listen to the words of the song again and take its message to heart.

Imagine a world where there were no *Walls*; where there was no hate, *fear*, hunger, or prejudice. Where we were all equal, despite the amount of money we made, our occupation, race, sex, or age. A world where we all treated each other with respect, care, compassion, empathy, and *unconditional love.* Instead of selfishness, we shared the bounties of the earth, so no one would ever be hungry again. Instead of destroying the earth carelessly and greedily, by polluting and warming our planet, we took care of the earth and treated it with the respect it deserves.

We can clean the planet, grow enough food for everyone, eliminate homelessness, share our medicines to cure treatable illnesses, and treat each other and all life with respect and *Love*. We have the technology right *now* to do all of these things; all we lack is the will.

Remember, *"the answers lie within, they always have. Look there first to find what you seek, and then share your love unconditionally with the world."*

We have a choice to make; it is our hope we will all choose wisely.

The first peace, which is the most important, is that which comes within

the souls of people

when they realize their relationship, their oneness, with the universe

and all its powers, and when they realize that at the center of the

universe dwells the Great Spirit,

and that this center is really everywhere,

it is within each of us.

~ Black Elk - Oglala Sioux

Chapter 10:

The Illusion of Happiness

The Illusion of Happiness

There are two ways to view Happiness.

One is from what we "Learned" it to be.

We were taught Happiness comes from making a lot of money,

Having a house, car, family, a lot of material possessions,

Doing things that will make "You" happy.

This type of happiness is "An Illusion of Happiness".

If we do all these things, are we truly happy?

The other type of Happiness comes from "Within", from our Spirit.

This kind of Happiness results from doing things "Selflessly"

benefiting others,

Bringing Happiness to "Everyone."

This type of happiness brings Inner Peace, Joy,

And many other positive feelings,

Including an understanding of the Meaning of Life.

We must each choose which form of Happiness to pursue.

It is my hope we choose wisely.

Throughout our lives, we strive to be happy. We have *learned* if we make a lot of money and have material possessions, we will be able to enjoy ourselves and be "successful" in life. We buy houses, cars, big TVs, nice furniture, branded clothes, and many other things we think will bring us happiness. When we are older, we may even travel to exotic places, go on cruises, drink alcohol, and take drugs, and more we have learned will make us happy as well. We get married, have children, and make friends as we know this will make our life complete. Yet despite all this, "*are we truly happy*"?

The Illusion of Happiness exists when we look for our happiness by doing all the things we "learned" will make us happy as we were growing up. After we are born, our "*education*" begins. We observe and learn from every interaction we have. By listening to our parents, teachers, and friends, we learn how to act around others so we will be liked. We read, watch movies, and surf the internet to learn about life, love, and everything we need to know to be "successful" in life.

We believe *the "Meaning of Life" is to share our Light and Love selflessly with everyone.* It is the difference in how we define love that will determine if our life is worthwhile and successful. We believe love and success many find in the world are an *Illusion* meant to distract us from the real answers we so desperately hope to find; those answers must first be found "*within.*" The *Meaning of Life* is to not only realize this but *accept* and *share* this knowledge with others. In a more *Spiritual* sense, the goal of life is to share our "*Light*" with the world and by doing so, to help others find their *Light* as well.

Changing our emotions is hard to do. Throughout our lives, we were *taught* what was "acceptable" and this became our norm. Though we feel terrible when we hear about atrocities where hundreds of thousands or millions die, we are grateful we are still alive, and this did not happen to us or anyone we love. We internalize these tragedies, but we know we cannot change anything. We therefore continue to live our life, trying to survive and be happy, despite all the horrors seen every day in the world.

We watch and we *learn* as people, lacking respect for each other, feel they are better and more deserving than others. We dehumanize each other as we strive for success in the world. We learn that we live in a competitive world, where money is the currency of success. We know we must look out for ourselves in order to survive, so we may be able to buy and have the things we need to be happy. We live our entire lives believing many of these things, yet for so many, the question that begs to be answered is: *Are we truly happy or is this just an "Illusion of Happiness"?*

If we search for "true" happiness and meaning in the world, it will never be found; almost everything we *learned* and believed will never lead to what we are truly searching for. If we accept the *Self's* version of life, though we may survive, live to an old age, be "successful," have a family and many friends, travel and own many nice things, there will always be a feeling deep *within* that something is missing or wrong. We may spend our entire life seeking happiness and, though we believe we may have "found it," we must ask ourselves if we truly have.

The message Bodhi and I hoped to share, by writing this book, is: *The Spirit exists within all life; hearing, accepting, and sharing "its message" during our life is the reason we are alive; it is the "Meaning of Life." The Spirit's message is often muted due the influence of the Self. Many of our problems, anxieties and illnesses are the direct result of the Spirit trying to "be heard" and the Self trying to suppress its message.*

The Self teaches us about Self-love. The Spirit, however, has a very different message. Its message has to do with Self-less Love. The Spirit teaches us respect, compassion, empathy, caring, selflessness, understanding, and much more. Its message is: we are all in life's journey together; only when all of us succeed will our lives have meaning. We are alive more than to just survive; there is a much deeper reason. Only by understanding and "accepting" this, can the "Illusion of Happiness" be shattered. Only by opening our hearts and helping each other, without expectation, will we find "true happiness" and meaning in our lives.

In our natural state, we are glorious beings.

In the world of illusion, we are lost and imprisoned,

slaves to our appetites and our will to false power.

~ Marianne Williamson

Chapter 11:

The Meaning of Life

Is There a "Reason We Are Alive"?

After we are born, we all ask that question sometime during our Lives.

Are we Alive just to "Survive", Idly passing time until we get old and

die?

If we make a lot of money, own many nice possessions, have a family,

Or anything else many would say is "our reason for life,"

When we prepare to die, would we feel our life was important and worthwhile?

Or is there more to our Journey Through Life?

Most are "Asleep", going through the motions, passing time,

Doing the many mundane things life offers until they die.

There are others, though, questioning if "There is Meaning" to life.

Beginning to sense, "Within," an unrelenting message,

"Waking" them from their deep slumber.

They begin to "Awaken" to the possibility

We are born for a Reason: to Learn, Share, Help Others Selflessly,

Reevaluating Everything we once believed to be true,

Beginning our Journey Towards "Enlightenment."

The choice which path in life we each take is Ours.

To "Sleep" through life or begin to "Wake up"

By "Listening" quietly to the messages Within.

By doing this, the "Reason We Are Alive" will become obvious.

Throughout history, many have searched for the "*Meaning of Life*."

Philosophers, religious leaders, scientists, and metaphysical observers, among others, have sought to answer a very simple question: "*Why are we alive?*"

People from different cultures may answer this question many ways. There are numerous theories that try to explain the *Meaning of Life*. Among these are those discussed by Plato, Aristotle, and other philosophers, as well as theories described by Nihilism, Pragmatism, Theism, Existentialism, Secular Humanism, Mohism, Confucianism, Taoism, Shintoism, Hinduism, Buddhism, and other schools of thought. To simplify this discussion, however, we will only consider two very general schools of thought when looking for our answer.

The first dogma believes in science, in only what can be "proved." They believe there is nothing before or after life, and after we die, we simply cease to exist. There is no God, spirit, or afterlife; death is final. Those who believe this also believe life does not have a spiritual meaning and meaning will only be found "empirically" while we are alive.

The other collective, however, is addressed in much more detail throughout history. Those in this group believe in *God, Spirit, Soul*, afterlife, and reincarnation, and believe, after we die, our *Spirit* leaves our body to be either reborn or travel to another plane of existence, with others, who have also reached *Enlightenment.*

This book cannot be complete unless we attempt to answer this question as well. Since this is the last chapter of the book, we will try to briefly summarize all we have talked about so far.

It is our belief there is a *Spirit,* an *Essence,* within every living thing and it is our *"purpose"* in life to *understand, accept, and share* this *Essence* with all others. We also believe the interactions between the *Self* and the *Spirit,* which are in constant conflict, are the cause of much of the strife and illness we experience throughout our lives.

The *Self* is created with our birth and teaches us how to *"survive"* in the world. Its "advice," which is frequently in opposition to that of the *Spirit,* often leads to unhappiness, anxiety, and stress. The *Self* may be described as a combination of many *learned* negative and *"perceived"* positive *(pseudo) emotions* we are *taught* and experience during our lifetime.

The *Spirit,* however, is eternal and lies *within* everything that has life; it even exists before we are born and after we die. Understanding, *accepting,* and sharing the message from your *"Higher Self"* (*Spirit*), is the reason we are alive, the *"Meaning of Life."* The *Spirit* encompasses all the pure positive emotions that have always been *within* us. We believe only by embracing the message of the *Spirit,* rather than the *Self,* will our lives truly have meaning. Though the *Self* is necessary for our daily survival in the world, without *accepting* the *Spirit* in our lives, our life will be incomplete.

The *Spirit* is here to guide and give our lives meaning. *Awakening* is understanding the *Spirit* exists. Though we know the *Spirit* is *within* everything that has life, *Enlightenment* will remain elusive until this knowledge is fully "*accepted.*" There are many in society who are *Awakened*, though they still search for their answers and happiness in the world around them. Thus, they have not *accepted* the role of the *Spirit* fully and therefore, *Enlightenment* eludes them.

In psychology, as well as in almost all disciplines based on science, since the *Spirit* cannot be scientifically proven, it is generally dismissed. It is our belief if this continues, as long as the *Spirit* is not fully *accepted,* the many struggles and illnesses we encounter throughout our life will continue. We suggest *the "Meaning of Life" has to do with listening, hearing, sharing, and following the guidance of your Spirit within.*

We spend our entire lives searching the world for the answer to two basic questions: "*Why are we alive?*" and "*What is the Meaning of Life?*" We search in many places throughout the world for the answers. We look to others to provide meaning; not finding it there, we believe meaning will be found if we are successful at work, make a lot of money, have many possessions, a family, other things we believe will make us "successful". Though we think we are "happy" and leading a successful life, it is our contention this happiness is temporary and an *"Illusion."*

We have been taught (socialized) from birth what happiness is. Yet, even if we are "successful" and leading a "happy" life, there are many days we slip back through the *Door*, which leads to *Enlightenment*, on top of the hill. We fall back down the hill, partially if not completely, and return to the realities and chaos of living and believing what we have been taught since the day we were born.

"The Illusion of Happiness" tells us the Meaning of Life cannot be found in the world or through being with others as we were taught. It may only be found with the acceptance of the Spirit and sharing its love selflessly with all others.

The secret of merging with Spirit and

recognizing the oneness of the whole Universe

cannot be learned in a lifetime,

but can be revealed in a moment,

for it has always lived within each and every one of us.

~ Jonathan Lockwood Huie

Epilogue

Treating the Mind ("Ego/Self") and Heart ("Spirit")

Psychology treats the "Mind" (Ego/Self), allowing us to return and

function in the world.

But is that enough?

Without also treating the "Heart" (Spirit), though we may be able to

survive in the world,

Does it truly treat the underlying cause of an illness?

There are some psychologists who "believe" they are treating the

"Heart",

But are they?

If they treat problems stemming from the Heart using techniques they

"Learned",

Their treatment is insufficient.

Though treating the "Mind" and "Learned" emotions stemming from

the Heart,

May "Appear" successful, are they?

Only by including the "Inherent" natural emotions residing within the

Heart,

Emotions we did not "Learn" but exist "Within" everyone before we

are born,

Will any treatment truly be successful?

These are the emotions giving our life "Meaning".

By not including the "Heart" in any treatment,

A return to a life of insignificance and mediocrity is all that can be

hoped for.

There are two paths we may take in life. The first is the path of the *Spirit*. This path may only be found *within* and is where the *Spirit/Soul/Essence/God* is found. Following this path leads to inner peace, finding deeper meaning, and is where *unconditional selfless love* exists. When viewing anxiety and depression in a "*Spiritual*" way, we believe these disorders are our *Spirit's* way of telling us we are on the wrong path and these problems are caused, at least partially, by the *Self* trying to reassert itself over the messages the *Spirit* is hoping to share.

The other path, containing everything we *learn* and are *taught* to be true after we are born, is the *"Self"* or *"Ego;" this path* contributes to many illnesses and to *all* of the problems observed throughout the world.

This epilogue is directed specifically towards all medical professionals who attempt to help others cope with the intense stress, anxiety, depression, and other related illnesses seen in the world today. We, too, believe it is important to confront issues that may arise from triggers and events that occurred in the past, to teach everyone coping skills to confront the challenges of living in the world, and to accept the need for counseling and medications, if needed, to help treat these illnesses.

While all of these things must be considered, if therapy is stopped here, your job is incomplete. The difference between a good doctor or therapist and an excellent one is that the former will help someone return to and survive in the world of the *Self,* while an excellent therapist will not only do that, but also redirect their patients onto a *Spiritual* path to "fully" treat their illness.

Could many of the illnesses we see, at least partially, be the result of the *Spirit*, behind its *Wall and Mask*, trying to *Awaken* us? When it attempts to do so, perhaps the *Self* triggers illnesses (psychiatric, psychosomatic, and medical) to "distract us" from the message it is trying to communicate? If we treat only the emotional or physical symptoms (Mind and Body) presented to us, and we continue to ignore the "*message*" from the *Spirit*, we are doing an injustice to those we seek to help. Unless the *Spirit* is included in the overall treatment, only an "*Illusion of Success,*" a partial incomplete treatment, is often achieved.

In this book, *The Illusion of Happiness: Choosing Love Over Fear*, we attempted to show the importance and benefit of including the *Spirit* in all treatments, in addition to traditional therapy. To what extent are illnesses caused or made worse by *Spiritual*, rather than emotional or physical problems? This question needs to be considered when a treatment plan is being devised. By including the *Spirit*, in addition to traditional therapy, the entire person will be treated. If we continue to follow only the current two-dimensional traditional therapies to treat illnesses, then, though there may be partial improvement, it is much more likely the apparent improvement will not be as long lasting or complete.

We wrote this book to share this knowledge and to emphasize the importance and need for inclusion of the *Spirit* in the treatment of many psychological, psychosomatic, and medical illnesses. We also hope to open our minds to the possibilities that will present themselves if we also accept the messages of the *Spirit*, rather than just of the traditional, *learned* treatments of the *Self*. The understanding of the *Mind, Body, Spirit Connection* can expose new directions in the treatment of illnesses ineffectively addressed by traditional means, which neglect the *spiritual* integration into the current mind, body approaches. An open mind will, therefore, be needed when reading this book, but the possibilities of improving outcomes are worth the risk.

We are asking you to take a *"Spiritual Leap of Faith"* to consider including the *Spirit* when any illness is treated. There is no downside or potential negative results in doing this. Rather, there is the possibility that a more complete, *Enlightened* connection and outcome will be found. This is a connection that will not only benefit the person being treated, but also those who are prescribing the treatment as well.

Together, we can and must make this a better world.

The Lie

As soon as we are born, the Lie begins.

Our Socialization teaches us to Accept the Mores of Society

And "Our" Importance in the world.

We learn those who are famous, wealthy, have important jobs,

A certain skin color, religion, sex or

Any other comparisons we "Learned" defined Superiority in the world,

Are more "Successful" and "Better" than others.

Nothing could be further from the truth.

In truth, our "Egocentric" upbring is

The Cause of Hatred, Greed, War, Climate Change, Murder,

Prejudice and so many other "Negative" problems

Present in the world both today and throughout history.

The Truth is "No One" is more important than another

Regardless of their "Accomplishments in Life."

What defines Truth is "Everyone's" Journey Through Life

Being as Valuable as our Own,

Sharing the resources of the planet Equally,

Allowing Every Life" to Flourish, be Important, Successful and

Meaningful.

Author's Note

It is our hope your Journey Towards Enlightenment has been enhanced by reading this Spiritual novel. If it has, could you *"Please"* take a few minutes to

"Write a Review"

and perhaps recommend this book on *Social Media* and to your *Friends and Family*. Bodhi and I wrote this book to try to *Awaken* and help others, who are *Awakened,* more fully understand what *Enlightenment* is, so their *Spiritual Journey Through Life* may be more fully realized.

Thank you for taking the time to read one of the books in *"The Awakening Tetralogy"*

Please spread our message, for we are all traveling life's journey

"together."

We hope you will also read all the books in "The Awakening Tetralogy":

"Today I Am Going to Die: Choices in Life"

"The Spirit Guide: Journey Through Life"

"Tranquility: A Village of Hope"

"The Illusion of Happiness: Choosing Love Over Fear"

{Please check out our website: **http://kenluball.com** to learn more about these books}

Feel free to Share your Thoughts & Questions about "Spirituality" with me @: **findingyourlight14@gmail.com**

Let's share our *Journey Through Life* together. Please check out my "**Blog & Website**" and Follow/Like/Friend me on "**Facebook, Instagram, You Tube, Twitter, Pinterest, LinkedIn & Reddit**".

ADDENDUM:

SPIRITUAL

REFLECTIONS

Embrace Love Over Fear

What is Learned during the first five years of a child's life,

May affect their "Entire Life."

The many struggles we have throughout our lives

Often result from the beliefs we developed

During these early, impressionable years,

And the "Acceptance" of the many false self-centered

Egocentric messages we received as the truth,

As we Learn our role in the world.

During these years if a child is taught

To view the world and others through a Dark Negative Prism,

One where "Fear" and concern for yourself,

Dominate "Love" and concern for the well-being of "Everyone",

The challenges these children will face will be great.

If, however, during these early years,

They embrace "Love Over Fear",

Concerned for the success and happiness of Everyone

Rather than only for themselves,

Their lives will take a much different direction.

These children will learn to understand,

Treat others and all life with respect,

And view life with Wonder and Awe,

Rather than with Fear and Hate.

It is time to change the paradigm of life

Living a Successful Life

Is "Success" living to old age, making a lot of money, having a

prestigious job,

A family, big house and being able to do the best things life has to

offer?

How many people have accepted this "Egocentric" definition of

success?

How many wealthy people, who have "Everything", are miserable and

in pain?

How many of us feel the same way, as we struggle, every day, through

life?

There is another definition of success though, one much less

recognized.

Success involves Sharing the inherent "Unconditional Love"

(Love given without expectation of receiving anything in return),

Selflessly With all Others.

Instead of wanting only "Success" for ourselves, we want it for

"Everyone".

The former definition for success leads to many challenges in life.

The latter leads to True Happiness, Inner Peace

And to having led a Meaningful "Successful" Life.

You are Never Truly Alone

We are each "Accompanied" through life by a Spirit Guide.

The answers we seek

Enabling us to embrace Inner Peace, Love and Meaning in our Life,

May "Never" be found in the World by looking outside

Or being with another person.

The answers may only be found looking "Within",

Where the Spirit Guide exists.

"Listen" quietly to the "Voice" you "Hear",

Then Share its message with All others.

What is Freedom?

We share our planet with many others.

Not only people, but animals, plants, and other forms of life as well.

Yet we treat each other and our planet as being Insignificant and

Unimportant.

Many are so concerned about "Their" freedom

They simply ignore all others, concerned only for what is Best for

themself.

By doing so, we are not only alienating ourselves from each other

But from what is best for all life on our planet and

Even for the survival of our planet itself.

Unless we change our definition of "Freedom"

To include treating All Life and the Earth with Equal respect

Caring for what is "Best" for "Everyone", not only "Ourselves"

The downward spiral of life will continue unabated,

Leaving our children to be raised in an

Unsustainable world of Fear and Hate.

Freedom is Equally Respecting and Treating All Life and Each Other

As we Ourselves wish to be treated.

It is time for each of us to decide "What is Freedom"?

It is my hope we choose the right answer.

Finding Happiness

We All wish to instill positive values in our children.

When our child is first born, we are Hopeful and Idealistic.

Caring, Being Respectful, Empathetic, Concerned for Others,

Accepting the importance of every life,

Are just a few of the positive Beliefs we encourage our children

To Learn when they are young.

How we raise our children, especially when they are very young,

As they are Socialized, "Taught" and "Learn" how to survive in the

world,

Often determines if they will find "Happiness" during their life.

If our children are "Taught" to Accept the Beliefs in the world,

Being concerned primarily for what is Best for Themselves,

Rather than the Positive values we first hoped they would learn

When they were first born,

Though they may be "Successful", become famous,

Wealthy, have many material possessions,

Are they truly "Happy"?

If, however, we raise our children to

Genuinely Accept and Embrace the values

We had hoped to share with them when they were young,

When they were first born, and we were still "Idealistic",

Perhaps they will not need to struggle to find Happiness,

Inherently "Understanding" Happiness

Does not come from "Anything" found in the world.

It only may be found "Within",

By Sharing the positive values our parents once hoped

We would Embrace when we were first born.

The Lesson We Are Here to Learn

When we die, the many challenges life had presented us end

As our physical body and Ego cease to exist.

Everything we accumulated during our lifetime

Will not accompany us, as we are "laid to rest".

It no longer will matter if you lived a "Successful" life,

Were wealthy, famous, had a prestigious job,

The color of your skin, male or female, gay or straight

Or any other comparison that can be made.

When we die, all that is left is an empty shell once housing our

Spirit/Soul.

Spirit is eternal, accompanying each of us, on our Journey Through

Life.

You "Awaken" when you begin to question

If everything you Learned while you were alive (Ego) is True.

You become "Enlightened" when you "Accept" None of it was.

"Selflessly Embracing" the Spirit's message while we are alive

Is the reason we are born, "The Meaning of Life".

Do not wait until you approach death to finally understand

The lesson we are here to Learn and

The Spiritual path we are meant to follow.

Let us use our time alive "Wisely",

"Accepting" and "Unconditionally Sharing" the positive Loving values

of the Spirit.

With this Embrace, will come Inner Peace

Knowing your life has been Meaningful and

Your Journey Through Life "Successful".

Every Life is Important, Equal and Connected

Inequality is frequently determined by where you are born,

If your family is rich or poor, the color of your skin, male or female,

Your sexual preference, religious beliefs, job, appearance, education,

Or any of the many other comparisons differentiating us from each

other.

Often, wanting to "Feel" Superior and more "Successful" than others

We treat and talk to others with "Disrespect" due to their differences,

Making us "Feel" we are Better than they are.

This is the cause of "All" man-made problems experienced throughout

time.

If you believe this "Illusion", continue following the same path

Pursued throughout millennia, "Nothing Will Change".

Wars, Hunger, Homelessness, Climate Change, Fear, Hate, Prejudice

And all the many other challenges experienced by so many

Will continue Unabated.

A radical change in Thinking and Actions is needed to alter this dynamic.

This transformation can only happen when there is

A Darwinian "Spiritual Evolution" of our planet.

One where we "Acknowledge" we "Never" have been Better or

Superior to another,

Helping All Others, Treating Each other with "Respect",

Accepting "Every" Life is Important, Equal and Connected.

Do No Harm

With Every decision we make during our life,

Our "Primary" guiding principle should be "Do No Harm".

Whether that harm is physical, emotional, verbal, financial

Or in any other manner, it does Not matter.

Every person, every form of life, deserves to be treated

With Respect and Empathy,

Always Considering what your behaviors, words and actions might

bring.

Be Thoughtful therefore "Before" you Act or Speak.

Our actions may Help others, though they may also cause great "Pain".

Let us All help bring change to the world

By adopting this one simple principle

And teaching it to our children,

And by doing so, help make

The world a more loving, caring home for them to live in.

Memories

Good Memories enrich our lives of wonderful times gone by.

They often bring a smile on our face as we

Remember the past when life was fun, and we were happy.

There are also Bad Memories as well though,

Haunting our dreams and actions, often happening

When something triggers a past event.

These Memories remind us of the many challenges we faced

As we struggled to survive and endure in an often-uncaring world.

These memories were both formed living in a world of uncertainty

And though the good memories may bring us happiness temporarily,

This happiness does not last, as the many daily struggles

We experience every day engulf us once more in life's daily

challenges.

There is a third type of Memory though, often not considered.

This type of Memory is Inherent, present already

In each of our cells, in our DNA, when we are first born.

This Memory is found in "Every" Life throughout the universe,

Emanating from the Spirit Within.

Remembering and Sharing the Message

Of Unconditional Love residing within the Spirit,

Gives Each Life Meaning and is the Reason we are born.

Unlike the brief feelings we experience

With the other two types of Memories,

Embracing the Inherent Spiritual Memories Within

Will bring "Lasting" Joy and Insight to our lives.

Sharing these Memories "Without Reserve" with All others

Will also bring Inner Peace, Enduring Happiness, and a

True Understanding of the "Meaning of Life".

Spirituality – Finding the Answers We Seek

Many seek answers in the many different religions created by man,

Though will "Not" find them there.

These religions long ago lost their significance and

Meaning, as they adopted Man's

Interpretation of right and wrong, good and evil,

And other man-made comparisons.

There is another path, however, for those seeking "Answers".

Spirituality is the belief there is a small piece of God (a Spirit or Soul)

"Within" each life, and

Therefore "Every" life is Sacred,

Deserving to be treated with "Unconditional" Respect and Love.

Spirituality is Innate, existing Within Every Life.

With the "Acceptance" of Spirituality comes

Wisdom, Compassion, Kindness, and Love for "All" Life.

Embracing Spirituality, Will bring the Answers we seek as well as

Inner Peace and Meaning to our lives.

Truth Lies "Within"

"Awakening" begins with gnawing doubts

Emanating from *Within* questioning the validity of

Everything we have been Taught

And "Accepted" to be true since our birth.

"Enlightenment" occurs with the realization and

"Acceptance" *Everything* we have Learned

In our life, that we had accepted as true, *"Was Not"*.

Truth Lies "Within"; it may Never be found anywhere else.

Our Journey Through Life

The Journey Through Life is often Long, Difficult and

At times Lonely, though can be very rewarding as well.

We each choose our direction through life,

Following either the Learned path

Or deciding to pursue the Spiritual Path instead.

"Accepting" all we are Taught and Believed is true,

Abiding by the status quo,

Fearful of challenging the dictates of society,

Leads to a life riddled with doubt, anxiety, and mediocrity.

The Journey Through Life, however, is Not predestined.

We may instead choose to venture off the "Accepted" path in life

Detouring "Inward", merging with our Spiritual Higher Self,

Leading to Love, Inner Peace, and a genuine Understanding

Of the "Meaning of Life".

What is Important in Life?

The time you have left as you approach death

Is an interesting time in your life.

Many things, once appearing to be important, no longer are.

You begin to realize life really is not complicated or complex.

Rather, it is quite simple.

The money, material possessions, job you had, and

Almost everything else you once thought defined

What a "Successful" life is, no longer matter.

Nothing will accompany you when you die.

You finally realize none of those things are important,

"Or Ever Were".

Don't wait until the end of your life to decide

What is truly important.

Live each day as if it was your last.

To discover what is Important,

Close your eyes, relax your mind and body, and

"Listen" to the quiet voice "Within."

Follow the suggestions you "Hear" (From your Spirit),

Accepting its advice whole-heartedly,

Living the rest of your life Selflessly helping others

In "Their" journey through life.

By doing so, when you near death,

You will have no regrets by having led a Meaningful life,

One full of True Love, Inner Peace and Happiness.

A Spiritual Evolution

Our thinking is dictated by the Ego,

What we "Learned" and "Accepted" as true

As we were indoctrinated and Socialized

To "Believe" societies traditions, mores, and customs.

Nothing will change if we continue

To follow this path through life.

Only when our Thinking, Beliefs and Actions are dictated

By our Spirit, "Within", may true change finally happen,

Leading to a Spiritual "Evolution" on our planet.

Our Real Emotions

The Ego or Self may give us the "*Illusion*" of Love and Happiness,

Though these feelings are false.

All "Learned" emotions are a Mirage.

Though they may seem real, "They Are Not".

The emotions associated with a truly "Happy" Meaningful Life

Come from the *Spirit* (our *Higher Self*).

Open your Heart, Freely Share your Love and Happiness

From "Within" with all others Unselfishly

To truly experience what these and all other

Positive emotions are Genuinely meant to feel like.

Lift the Veil

When You Open Your Eyes, what do you see?

Do you see Light or Darkness?

Light comes from "Within", viewing life as Loving, Hopeful,

Seeing the positive in every person and experience.

Darkness, however, comes from "Accepting"

The negative views and beliefs we "Learned" about the world.

To change the future, we must all "Lift the Veil"

Covering our eyes, Sharing our Light Within,

Allowing it to shine brightly for all to see.

We can change the world.

"*Listen*" to the quiet voice

"Within" our Heart,

Sharing its Selfless message

With everyone.

All life is Sacred and Precious

Respect All life and Mother Earth.

Have empathy, be humble, truthful and

Considerate of everyone.

Only by caring and helping each other

Will All our lives become not only easier

But more Meaningful as well.

We Are Never Alone

"Listen", "Hear", "Share".

"Listen" to the soft whispers within.

"Hear" its message of Love.

"Share" your Love freely with All.

It is everyone's responsibility to Help

Each other,

Easing Each of Our Journey Through Life.

The Mind, Body, Spirit Connection

Psychologists and Counselors enable us to return and function in

society,

But, often, their two-dimensional approach,

Treating only the Mind & Body, is deficient and inadequate.

Without also treating the Spiritual part of an illness,

The treatment is incomplete.

"The Spirit gives our Lives Meaning".

Without also treating the Spirit,

The result is a return to mediocrity.

The constant internal struggle between the Mind & Body and the Spirit,

Contributing to the symptoms of many disorders, continues,

Allowing the illness to not be fully treated and return.

The Spirit Must therefore be included in the treatment of Psychiatric

illnesses,

As well as many Psychosomatic and Medical illnesses as well.

Spirituality vs Religion

Spirituality is quite different from Religion.

Religion is created by man.

It may have had good intentions when it began,

But "Learned" beliefs and intentions are False.

Spirituality comes from "Within", where the Inherent beliefs of

God/Spirit/Soul, or whatever you may call it, Exists.

These are the Pure Whole Emotions "We Were Meant to Share and

Live By".

Whereas Religion divides us, Spirituality joins us together

To improve the life of All.

Our Search for Meaning

When we begin to search for Meaning in Our Life

Questioning the truth of all we were taught,

We begin to "*Awaken* and start the arduous journey

On the path towards *Enlightenment.*

This journey is long, often lonely, and quite challenging.

Only a few will reach the end of the path.

The journey often is not a choice for those who pursue it.

There is a gnawing unrelenting feeling "Within" that can no longer be

ignored.

This feeling comes from the "*Spirit*",

Questioning All the choices and everything we had been taught

And "Accepted" as true throughout our life.

At this moment, we "*Awaken*".

From this moment forward, your life will be changed forever.

You begin to question the friendships, job, marriage, and everything in

your life

As you embark on this new journey with those

Continuing to "Live" in an Unenlightened world.

God

The belief in God influences many people throughout the world.

Therefore, the awareness of God must not be ignored.

Whether you call God Spirit, Soul, or any other name,

This ethereal being has been the subject

Of much discussion throughout time.

Though God should unite us, often it does not.

All life, regardless of religion or any existing beliefs, is Important.

No one life is more important than another.

There is a small piece of God is "Within" every life,

Connecting each life to the other.

It is only when we "Share" this part of us "Selflessly"

"Unconditionally" with each other,

Will the Spiritual Evolution of our planet finally be realized.

A Time for Change

We have the ability to feed the hungry, clothe and house the needy,

Provide fresh water to the thirsty, treat most illnesses,

End climate change, war, intolerance, and many other challenges

"Now".

We must No longer accept these things as an irrefutable part of life.

It is time to alter this paradigm, ushering in a Spiritual Evolution,

Changing our dysfunctional world before it is too late,

For the survival and benefit of all life on our planet.

The Hope of Every Generation

When we were young, it was the greatest of times.

We believed we would change the world,

But did we?

If we look at the world today,

The answer most certainly must be "No".

We fell into a pattern so many generations do.

Trying to survive in the world,

We forgot the importance of Caring about each other Selflessly.

We eventually "accepted" society's egocentric definition of Success &

Happiness.

It is NOT too late, though, to open our hearts and share our Love

Unconditionally with all others.

By doing so, we can change the direction of the world,

Helping Everyone Succeed,

Leaving the world a better place for our children and each other.

Every person can change the world.

We each have, "Within" us, the Means to do so.

It begins by "Listening" quietly, "Accepting"

The messages you "Hear"

Then Sharing your "Light" with the World.

Love

Everyone wants love. Regardless of who you are, this one emotion

Has been desired throughout recorded history.

Yet it is your definition of Love that will decide if you will truly find it.

There are two ways to look at love.

One, is what we "Learned" love was as we were growing up,

By watching TV, reading books, and observing those around us.

"Learned Love" is conditional. It is given with the expectation

We will get something back in return; often this is the return of love

back.

The other way to view love is "Inherent Love".

This love comes from "Within" and is given freely and selflessly

Without expectation of receiving anything in return.

This "pure" form of love comes from our "Spirit/Soul"

And is what Love is meant to be and feel like.

To be able to discover Inherent Love, you need to be truly concerned

About "Everyone's" success in life, rather than only your success.

Simply looking at the world today and throughout history,

It is obvious what form of love is dominant.

It is up to each of us to spread Love "Selflessly",

To care equally for everyone's success in life,

For the Spiritual Evolution of our species to occur.

If we do not, the world we are leaving our children is destined for

failure.

Within

Within everything alive there is an "Essence".

Whether you call this Essence Spirit/Soul/God or anything else

It does not matter.

It is an Ethereal presence connecting all life together,

Giving our lives "Meaning".

"Awakening" happens when we first sense this presence

Is truly there and may be important in our life.

"Enlightenment" is reached when we "Accept"

It is more important than the "Ego",

Which encompasses everything we have Learned and

Believed to be True since we were born.

We finally understand the importance of "Every" life

Not just "Our" own life,

As the "Meaning of Life" finally becomes clear.

Our Children's Legacy

The older generations, all hopeful when we were young, "Failed".

Our failure is allowing our children to grow up in a World of

Fear, Greed, Prejudice, Inequality, Hatred, Hunger, Homelessness

Climate Change, War and Distrust.

Instead of "Helping Each Other", without pause,

As "Life is Meant to be Lived",

We focus only on Our Survival and "Success".

To change this paradigm,

To make this world "Safer" for our Children to grow up in,

It will take a Darwinian Shift of Consciousness,

Embracing Love over Fear by

Considering what is best for "Everyone" rather than only for Ourselves.

We are Not Alone

We are "All" here to help each other on our Journey Through Life.

Reach out when you are down.

We will help pick you up and gently guide you

To the path you are meant to follow.

This is what we were always meant to do,

To truly care about each other; helping each other "Selflessly".

By Sharing our Love Unconditionally with others,

Our lives will be Meaningful and

An Inner Peace will replace the Chaos dwelling Within.

Our Baggage in Life

Each one of us has "Baggage"

We carry from our Experiences in Life.

Our Baggage often causes us to see the World differently.

If your Baggage causes you to view the World with "Fear",

Concerned only for yourself and family,

Your narrowed Vision of Life

Will cloud many of your decisions

And lead to an "Unfulfilled" life.

If, however, "Despite" the Baggage you have carried in your life,

You embrace and live your life with "Love",

Shared Freely and Unconditionally with all others,

Your expanded Vision of Life

Will allow you to "Awaken",

Bringing Happiness, Inner Peace

And a True Understanding of the "Meaning of Life".

Which Truth Will We Teach Our Children?

As we are "Socializing" our Children, especially early in their lives,

It is important to Always be truthful and honest with them.

The question we each must ask ourselves is:

"What is the Truth"?

To simplify this discussion, assume there are only two types of truth.

The first type of truth teaches our Children to "Accept" the beliefs

Of the world as they are now and have been for millennia.

This truth emphasizes the individual, on what is Best for "Themselves,"

Accepting the idea of living in a world of competition and distrust,

Being concerned only for "Their" survival and happiness.

The other type of truth, however, has a very different view of life.

This truth emphasizes the collective, on what is Best for "Everyone,"

Accepting the idea of cooperation and trust, Selflessly Helping

Each other so Everyone may Succeed in their Journey Through Life.

Most of the problems seen in the world result from living in

An Egocentric world concerned only for what is best for "Ourselves".

All previous generations "Eventually" have embraced this type of

world.

It is a world of Fear, Hatred, Prejudice, Poverty, Homelessness,

Climate Change, Hunger, War, Cynicism, ad infinitum,

That will await our Children when they grow up.

We may only change this preordained future, by raising

The latest generation of children to be Selfless,

Unconditionally Sharing their Love Within with All others,

Assuring Everyone's survival and success in life.

One truth will lead to Struggle, maintaining the status quo.

The other truth will lead to "Enlightenment".

The only question we each must ask ourselves is:

Which Truth Will We Teach Our Children?

Including the Spirit in Treatment of "All" Illnesses

By adding the "*Spirit*" into the Mind-Body equation

A whole new world of possibilities for treatment of many

Psychiatric, Psychosomatic and Medical illnesses is opened.

Unlike the *Ego (Mind),* which is rooted in "*Fear*",

The *Spirit* is rooted in "*Love*".

Treating just the Mind and Body may allow someone to return

And function in society.

"Is that enough though"?

The "Spirit" gives our lives "Meaning".

Rather than continuing to only use the current Mind-Body approach

Of many medical practitioners,

By including the *Spirit* in the healing process as well for All illnesses,

New improved avenues for treatment may be discovered,

Making the treatments more Successful and Long-Lasting.

How to Raise a Happy Child

Bring up children to believe in the goodness of life,

To share Selflessly, Foster Respect and

Love for all others,

Regardless of any perceived learned differences

We are taught and accept as true.

Teach our children to find their path and Happiness in life,

Not in the world, but from their Spirit *"Within"*.

Then to share that Love Unselfishly

Our Future

To change the world, it is important to begin with our children.

Teaching them to live their lives with Love rather than Hate,

Curiosity rather than Fear, Acceptance rather than Prejudice,

Selflessness rather than Selfishness.

If the next generation of children are brought up this way,

Then perhaps it will not be too late

To change our destiny and our future.

Happiness, Love and Meaning

We all, on our journey through life,

Seek Happiness, Love and Meaning.

Whether these wonderful attributes are found, however,

Depend on where you are seeking them.

Though many, having achieved "Success" during their life,

Having wealth, a home, family, and many material possessions,

"Believe" they found Happiness, Love and Meaning,

They have simply bought into the "Illusion",

The "Learned" myth these things may be bought or found in the world.

"They Cannot".

In truth, Happiness, Love and Meaning must "First" be found Within

each of us

And then, will only be realized, by Sharing it selflessly with others.

Embrace the Good

Do you see the good in others or do you seek out their faults?

Do you have a need to prove you are better than another or

Can you accept the unique majesty of others?

Though there are many man made problems existing throughout the

world,

We each have a choice how we treat others.

Do not judge another, rather accept every life,

Embracing the uniqueness and Love within others.

Look for the good, discard the rest.

Help all those in need with kindness and empathy.

By doing so, we can not only change ourselves,

But we can change the future of the world itself.

A Part of Us

Within every life there is a Spirit/Soul/Essence/God.

It does not matter what you call it.

It Connects all of us to each other.

This part of us represents our "Higher-Self",

The genuine *Love*, within each life,

Meant to be shared with all others.

With every interaction, regardless how brief,

We share a small part of our Spirit with another,

Changing both your and their life forever.

Even if we physically die,

This encounter, despite how fleeting, will live within them in

perpetuity,

Enriching each in their journey through life.

"Accepting" this, sharing this part of us selflessly with others

Is "Enlightenment", the reason we are born,

The lesson we are here to learn,

The "Meaning of Life".

Pain

The emotional pain many feel is the cause

Of anxiety, stress, depression and most other

Challenges we each face in life as we strive

To survive and find joy and happiness in our lives.

This pain is caused by our "Learned" reactions to

Different things and situations we are or

Have been exposed to during our life.

We do Not have to confront every trauma or negative event

In our life to diminish this pain.

We only need to recognize the pain is caused

By following the wrong path through life;

The path we were taught to believe and accepted

As real as we were growing up.

To change our path, to rid ourselves of the pain,

To find true happiness and meaning in our lives,

Quiet your mind, "Listen" and

Follow the advice you "Hear".

The reason we are alive,

The Meaning of Life,

Is to listen quietly to the Spirit within and

Follow the path it leads you on.

Spirituality is the belief there is a

Piece of God (a Spirit or Soul) within each life,

And, because of this,

Every Life is Important, Equal, and Connected.

Reflections at the Twilight of Life

My body has become frail.

I am unable to do the things I used to do.

I now spend most of my time remembering my life,

And reflecting about life in general.

When I look at the world, I wonder why?

Why is there war, indiscriminate killing, starvation, hunger,

Homelessness, prejudice, hate, fear, climate change, inequality,

And daily struggles for so many that seem to never end?

Why are some people who are "Successful" in life,

Have a prestigious job, wealth, and many material possessions,

Unable to find inner peace, happiness, or meaning in their lives?

And others, who appear to have very little,

Are truly happy, and able to experience genuine inner peace?

Sitting on my porch, after much contemplation,

I believe I finally can answer this question.

Those who look to the world and others for their Happiness,

Meaning, and Success, who are primarily concerned for only their well-

being,

Struggle "Within" to find these things.

They also contribute to many of the problems

Experienced living in a self-centered uncaring world.

Those, however, who are brought up with Love,

Having respect and equal concern for every life

Will help eradicate many of the man-made problems above

Allowing not only their but all other lives to flourish

And have Meaning as well.

"About Ken"

Peace, Love & Light.

****

My name is Ken Luball. Spiritual Seeker ~ Author ~ Guide.

****

Author of "The Awakening Tetralogy: A series of Four Spiritual Books".

****

Ever since I was a young child, I knew my purpose in life; it was for me to Awaken, find Enlightenment, and share my experience and knowledge with others. To reach those lofty aspirations though, I first had to navigate through quite a few unexpected detours in my life.

Though I was brought up in a religious family, it did not help me *Hear* the messages from my *Spirit Guide, Bodhi.* If anything, religion only further isolated me, teaching me to accept the *Ego's* view of religion rather than *Bodhi's.* It was not until after I stopped following a formal religion, I finally was able to embrace *Spirituality,* and with this embrace, I *Awoke.*

Spirituality is the belief there is a piece of God (a *Spirit*) within everything that has life, and, because of this, all life is important, equal, and connected. After I *Awoke,* no longer having the dogma of religion handicapping my views, I was suddenly free to explore this philosophy of life more deeply. Only then did I become aware of the *Mask* I wore and the impenetrable *Wall* I had erected around my Heart; the *Mask* and *Wall* allowed me to survive in the world. I would always smile, appear happy, though, I would often feel intense anxiety within. This was something I never really understood until the moment I confronted my *Ego.* Little did I know, these survival mechanisms would have a profound effect on me for the majority of my life. By protecting me from emotional pain, they also isolated me from my family, everyone else in my life, and even from myself. No one could hurt me because I did not allow anyone to get close enough to do so. In turn, no one could love me or was I able to truly love another either. This superficial life, one devoid of risk or pain, left me *alone* in a sea of people.

It took many years before the first cracks in my *Wall* formed and before I could loosen the *Mask* I constantly wore. It took me almost an entire lifetime to become to be *Awakened* and begin my journey towards *Enlightenment.*

After I was clearly able to "*hear*" my *Spirit Guide, Bodhi*, I realized everything I had *Learned* from my *Ego* throughout my life was untrue. I had looked for love and happiness in the job I had, the money I made, things I owned, and through my wife and children. With the exception of the latter, I finally realized none of those things truly mattered. This does not mean I am ungrateful to my *Ego,* however. It taught me coping skills and allowed me to "succeed", or at least what I was taught success was. Though my *Ego* still remains with me, it has taken a more secondary position in my life now, relinquishing its former primary role to *my Spirit Guide, Bodhi.*

Decisions were now required. While it was tempting to take this newly found state of being and withdraw from society and all the hate, fear, cruelty, poverty, and greed that plagues it, I knew within myself this gift of Enlightenment was to be shared with others. That is my destiny. Therefore, I have written "The Awakening Tetralogy", a series of four "Spiritual" books, to share this knowledge with as many others as possible. It is my and Bodhi's *hope you will read these books, and in doing so, begin a new adventure. One where you will* Awaken *and further your journey towards* Enlightenment *with your Spirit Within.*

I do not know if our books will be read widely in my lifetime, though I hope one day they may help others Awaken and find Enlightenment as well.

"We are all on a Spiritual Journey of Love & Peace; together may we spread "Light" throughout the world"

***

Ken Luball is a Spiritual Seeker ~ Author ~ Guide on a mission to help Awaken as many people as possible. Born and raised in the US, Ken has had a lifelong obsession with finding the true Meaning of Life, and with his Spirit Guide, Bodhi, has successfully penned a tetralogy of stories, anecdotes, and lessons he has learned along the way. When he is not writing, Ken can be found enjoying 70's era classic rock and roll and folk music, hiking, interacting with his substantial social media following, and instilling the message of true joy into the hearts of his family and others.

To read more of Ken's life-changing reflections visit his Website: http://kenluball.com or reach out to him at findingyourlight14@gmail.com .

Made in United States
Orlando, FL
13 April 2022

16661992R10115